ACLS for

EMT-Basics

ACLS for

EMT-Basics

American Academy of Orthopaedic Surgeons

Author:
Mike Smith, MICP
Program Chair
Emergency Medical and Health Services
Tacoma Community College
Tacoma, WA

JONES AND BARTLETT PUBLISHERS

Sudbury, Massachusetts

BOSTON   TORONTO   LONDON   SINGAPORE

Jones and Bartlett Publishers

World Headquarters
Jones and Bartlett Publishers
40 Tall Pine Drive, Sudbury, MA 01776
978-443-5000
info@jbpub.com
www.EMSzone.com

Jones and Bartlett Publishers Canada
2406 Nikanna Road
Mississauga, ON CANADA L5C 2W6

Jones and Bartlett Publishers International
Barb House, Barb Mews
London W6 7PA, UK

Production Credits
Chief Executive Officer: Clayton E. Jones
Chief Operating Officer: Donald W. Jones, Jr
Executive V.P. and Publisher: Robert Holland
Director of Sales and Marketing: William J. Kane
V.P. Production and Design: Anne Spencer
V.P. Manufacturing and Inventory Control: Therese Bräuer
Publisher, Emergency Care: Kimberly Brophy
Emergency Care Associate Editor: Carol Brewer
Senior Production Editor: Linda S. DeBruyn
Text Design: Studio Montage
Cover Design: Nesbitt Graphics, Inc.
Editorial Production Service: Nesbitt Graphics, Inc.
Cover Photograph: © Bruce Ayres/Stone/Getty Images
Text Printing and Binding: Courier Company
Cover Printing: Lehigh Press

American Academy of Orthopaedic Surgeons

Editorial Credits
Vice President, Education Programs: Mark W. Wieting
Director, Department of Publications: Marilyn L. Fox, PhD
Managing Editor: Lynne Roby Shindoll
Senior Editor: Barbara A. Scotese
Associate Senior Editor: Susan Morritz Baim

Board of Directors 2002
Vernon T. Tolo, MD, *President*
James H. Herndon, MD
Robert W. Bucholz, MD
E. Anthony Rankin, MD
Andrew J. Weiland, MD
Edward A. Toriello, MD
Richard H. Gelberman, MD
S. Terry Canale, MD
Stephen A. Albanese, MD
Stephen P. England, MD
James N. Weinstein, DO
Gerald R. Williams, Jr, MD
Peter C. Amadio, MD
David G. Lewallen, MD
Glenn B. Pfeffer, MD
Lowry Jones, Jr, MD
Maureen Finnegan, MD
Peter J. Mandell, MD
William W. Tipton, Jr, MD *(ex officio)*

This textbook is intended solely as a guide to the appropriate procedures to be employed when rendering emergency care to the sick and injured. It is not intended as a statement of the standards of care required in any particular situation, because circumstances and the patient's physical condition can vary widely from one emergency to another. Nor is it intended that this textbook shall in any way advise emergency personnel concerning legal authority to perform the activities or procedures discussed. Such local determinations should be made only with the aid of legal counsel.

Library of Congress Cataloging-in-Publication Data
Smith, Mike
   ACLS for EMT-Basics / Mike Smith; American Academy of
Orthopaedic Surgeons.
      p.cm.
   Includes index.
   ISBN 0-7637-1505-0
   1. Cardiovascular emergencies. 2. Cardiac resuscitation. 3. Emergency medical technicians. I. Smith, Mike (Michael Gordon), 1952- II. American Academy of Orthopaedic Surgeons. III. Title.

   RC675.A253 2003
   616.1'025—dc21
                                                      2002034055

Additional credits appear on page 120 which constitutes a continuation of the copyright page.

Printed in the United States of America
06 05 04 03 02   10 9 8 7 6 5 4 3 2 1

Contents

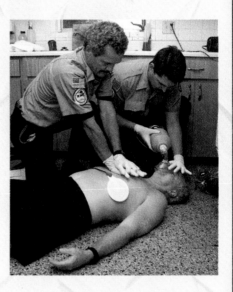

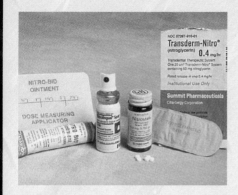

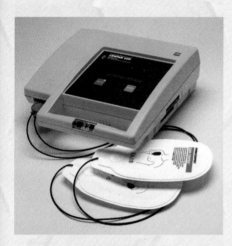

Preface

Many times, EMT-Basics (EMT-Bs) are placed in positions that require them to assist Advanced Life Support (ALS) providers, but the necessary tasks are not part of their initial EMT-B training. The ACLS for EMT-Basics program was developed to provide EMT-Bs with a knowledge base that will not only make them feel more comfortable in the ALS setting, but also allow them to become primary participants in the care of the ALS patient.

I have educated approximately 500 EMTs in ALS for BLS workshops over the last 10 years. Over the last few years I have had the pleasure of partnering with Mike Smith in these workshops.

Mike Smith is one of the foremost educators in EMS. Mike Smith has the ability to take a complicated subject and communicate it to students in a way that is simple to understand and retain. He has taken some of the most difficult objectives in ALS and provided them to you in this book in a simple and understandable format.

I am extremely proud of this book and the work that Mike Smith has provided for you. I know that once you have finished this book, you will find yourself not only more prepared for the ALS clinical setting, but also able to fulfill an integral role in the care of ALS patients.

Baxter Larmon, PhD, MICP
Professor of Medicine
UCLA School of Medicine
Director
UCLA Center for Prehospital Care
Inglewood, CA

Dedication:

This book is dedicated to Sylvia, Schmidt, and Missi for their unswerving support and endless encouragement.

Acknowledgments

Jones and Bartlett Publishers would like to thank the following people for reviewing this text.

Brenda M. Beasley, RN, BS, EMT-P
Calhoun Community College
Wedowee, AL

Elizabeth Criss, RN, CEN, MAEd
University Medical Center
Tucson, AZ

Jay Hafter, REMT-P, MS, JD
Foundation for Emergency Medical Research
University Heights, OH

Anita Huey, MS, RD, LD
Martin's Point Health Education
Portland, ME

Connie J. Mattera, MS, RN, EMT-P
Northwest Community EMSS
Arlington Heights, IL

Stephen J. Rahm, NREMT-P
Department of Combat Medic Training
Fort Sam Houston, TX

Rose Marie Tiernan, NREMT-B
EMT-B Lead Instructor
School Bergen County EMS Training Center
Paramus, NJ

Walk-Through

ACLS for EMT-Basics

Although EMT-Basics are not trained to provide advanced cardiac life support (ACLS), there is much they can do to improve the quality of management and thus the patient's chance for survival in a cardiac emergency.

When the EMT-Basic in the field is faced with the decision of whether or not to request a Paramedic unit, and when the Paramedic unit arrives, the EMT-Basic will be a more integral part of the team due to the base knowledge attained from this program. This text can be used in an ACLS training course for EMT-Basics, or as a supplement in an EMT-Basic course.

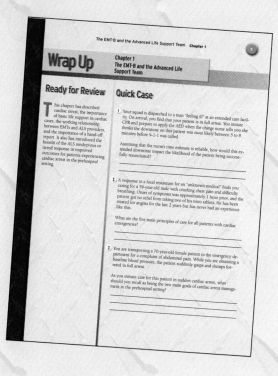

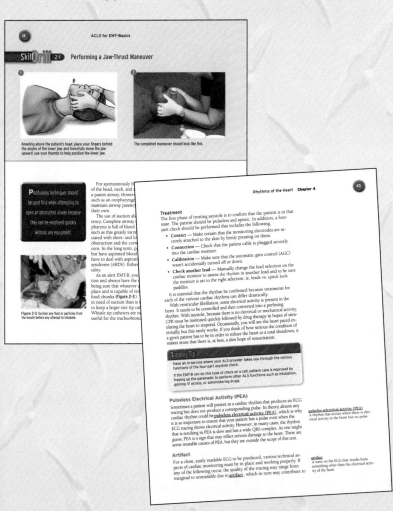

Special Features

- Quick Cases—Brief case studies accompanied by critical thinking questions that appear at the end of each chapter.
- Training Tips—Boxed tips that emphasize how EMT-Basics can further their understanding of ACLS.
- Key points are emphasized in the margin.
- Key terms are bolded and underlined in the text, then defined in the margin and also in the glossary at the end of the book.
- BLS skills related to ACLS care are presented in a step-by-step format.

http://acls.EMSzone.com

Online resources including key term flashcards, an online glossary, and web links are available at http://acls.EMSzone.com/.

Chapter 1

The EMT-B and the Advanced Life Support Team

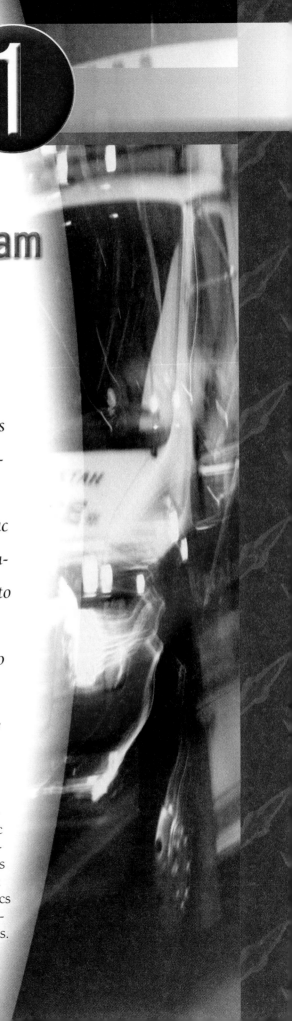

The purpose of this ACLS for EMT-Bs course is to make you, as a practicing EMT-B, a more valuable member of the emergency medical services (EMS) team. This course builds on the foundation of your initial EMT-B education by introducing or expanding your existing knowledge relative to the fundamentals of cardiac pharmacology, cardiac electrophysiology and ECG interpretation, endotracheal intubation, and defibrillation/cardioversion. You will learn how to contribute further to patient care in the areas mentioned above. While completion of this course will not certify you to perform _advanced cardiac life support (ACLS)_ skills in the field, you will become a more knowledgeable member of any EMS team and be able to provide improved patient care.

You will develop an appreciation of the principles and practices of advanced cardiac life support, especially as they relate to emergency cardiac care. With an appreciation of these principles, you will see how the combination of advanced life support (ALS) and basic life support (BLS) skills and teamwork can improve the survival rates of the patients we serve. At the completion of this course, you will be a greater asset to the paramedics and other members of the ALS team—not just during cardiac arrest management but whenever you are caring for patients with cardiac conditions.

Sudden Cardiac Arrest

During the next year, approximately 1 million people will experience the most serious of all medical emergencies—**sudden cardiac arrest**. Their hearts will stop beating, and without emergency cardiac intervention, they will die. Some patients will have diseased hearts that have little ability to survive such an event. Others may have healthy hearts that have stopped for some electrical or other imbalance in early and tragic sudden cardiac arrest. Almost all will result in a call to 9-1-1.

Emergency cardiac care is the application of the principles of emergency medicine focused specifically on the patient with a cardiac-oriented problem. When sudden cardiac arrest occurs, basic emergency cardiac care (BLS) provided by the EMS team coupled with ACLS may enable the team to resuscitate the patient, reverse the condition, and return the patient to a normal productive life. Keep in mind, however, that these actions and interventions make up a series of events that work together in parallel and in sequence to resuscitate the patient. If you consider the following emergency situations, you will see clearly how the outcomes might have been different if an EMT-B with a knowledge of cardiac care had been there to take the appropriate actions and applied interventions in the correct sequence as the EMT-B and ALS teams worked together.

- A patient in cardiac arrest has a blocked airway that is not opened; resuscitation is unsuccessful.
- A patient in sudden cardiac arrest in ventricular fibrillation waits 8 minutes for an **automated external defibrillator (AED).** When the machine arrives and is applied, the patient's heart does not respond.
- A patient in cardiac arrest is treated with BLS, but ALS is not available. Cardiopulmonary resuscitation (CPR) is continued for 25 minutes during the patient's transport to the hospital, but upon arrival at the emergency department, the physician declares the patient dead.

ALS and the EMT-B

Ask any seasoned EMS veteran about the first cardiac arrest he or she worked in the field, and chances are he or she remembers it, often with remarkable detail. For many, the situation represented the first practical application and real test of the theories and concepts they were taught during their initial training and education in the classroom. As that first code started to unfold, it quickly became apparent that his or her acquired knowledge had to transform into practical application or the patient would certainly die.

It is an unfortunate fact that less than 5% of all patients who experience sudden cardiac arrest out of the hospital survive. This means that most of your attempts at resuscitating a patient in sudden cardiac arrest will not return the heart to normal rhythm, and your efforts will not bring the patient back to life. This harsh reality does not mean that you should abandon all attempts at resuscitation. Rather, you should understand *why* most patients die and learn how to respond to cardiac emergencies effectively. Your focus should be on improving your knowledge and skill level to improve the outcome for patients in cardiac arrest.

---

advanced cardiac life support (ACLS)
The provision of emergency cardiac care using invasive techniques or technology.

sudden cardiac arrest
A state in which the heart fails to generate an effective and detectable blood flow; pulses are not palpable in cardiac arrest even if muscular and electrical activity continues in the heart.

emergency cardiac care
The principles of emergency medicine focused specifically on a patient with a cardiac-oriented problem.

automated external defibrillator (AED)
A small computerized defibrillator that analyzes electrical signals from the heart to determine when ventricular fibrillation is taking place and then administers a shock to defibrillate the heart.

The window of time for resuscitating a cardiac patient without causing brain damage is small. For the best outcome, procedures must be performed in the appropriate sequence within the appropriate time frame.

Besides the potential of the patient's death, there is the possibility of brain damage. It is tragic when our resuscitation efforts save the patient's life yet result in permanent damage to the brain. More than 10 years ago, EMS pioneer Peter Safar proposed changing the term CPR to CPCR (cardiopulmonary cerebral resuscitation) as a reminder that the brain, along with the heart and lungs, is an integral component in the resuscitation process.

Because a cardiac arrest causes permanent damage to the brain more quickly than to other parts of the body, there is a shorter span of time to resuscitate the patient and prevent brain damage. If the brain is damaged, there may be little remaining but the physical shell of who the person once was. The personality, emotions, hopes, and dreams are either permanently altered, or, in the worst case, cease to exist, as with patients deemed "brain dead."

Medical science is unable to predict which patients will be resuscitated. For patients who survive a sudden cardiac arrest, the goal for recovery is to return as closely as possible to their former self and lifestyle. When confronted with a sudden cardiac arrest, each member of the EMS team must focus on doing the right things, in the right sequence, and in the right time frame.

BLS and ALS: The Team Approach

It is essential to understand that in the world of prehospital emergency care, BLS and ALS cannot exist without each other. BLS interventions may prevent sudden cardiac arrest, and if sudden cardiac arrest occurs, BLS can keep oxygen going into the lungs and blood flowing to the brain and other organs until ALS measures can be instituted to reverse and stabilize the patient's condition. Conversely, the techniques and technology of ALS become meaningless if the patient is pulseless and apneic for 8 to 10 minutes and the brain irreversibly damaged prior to ALS arrival. Bringing BLS and ALS together in a seamless patient care effort requires focused effort, excellent communication skills, and teamwork. Each member of the EMS team must work in harmony with one goal in mind—quality patient care (**Figure 1-1**).

> **W**hen dealing with cardiac emergencies, teamwork between BLS and ALS personnel is essential.

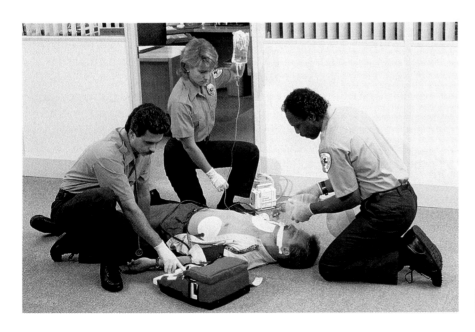

Figure 1-1 Members of the EMS team must work together to provide quality patient care.

ALS rendezvous
A model for patient care in which the BLS team receives the call and arranges for ALS providers to meet them at an agreed-upon location, resulting in providing ACLS care to the patient as soon as possible.

tiered response
Dispatch of both ALS and BLS to the same call. May involve an ALS rendezvous.

More and more BLS service providers are working to implement **ALS rendezvous** or **tiered response** models. With these approaches, the goal is to get the ALS team to the patient as fast as possible, allowing for better patient outcomes. In these models, the BLS team receives the call. En route to the patient, the BLS team or its dispatcher immediately calls the ALS providers. Depending on the distance involved, there are two options. Either both teams will proceed to the patient site (or rendezvous there), or the BLS team will go to the patient, provide life support, and transport the patient to a site closer to the ALS team.

By getting the two tiers of support started at the time of the first call, the BLS team allows the patient a better chance of survival by preparing for the next level of care. Through integration of BLS and ALS skills, it is possible to deliver the same quality of care available in both urban and rural settings.

Goals for Patient Care

There are many ways for you and your team to improve patient survival rates. This should be the goal that drives BLS and ALS providers. All that we do in prehospital medicine—every new technique, new intervention, protocol change, and standing order revision—should be motivated by a single question: Is this in the best interest of patient care? Only when the answer is "yes" will we truly be meeting the needs of our patients. With all this as the setting for your acquisition of additional knowledge and skills, let's get to the basics of emergency cardiac care.

Whenever you are providing care to a cardiac patient, your energies should focus on the following (**Figure 1-2**):

- Reducing patient anxiety and decreasing pain
- Preventing **hypoxia**
- Preventing (but staying alert for) lethal arrhythmias
- Maintaining adequate perfusion
- Reducing the incidence of out-of-hospital cardiac arrest

hypoxia
A dangerous condition in which the body tissues and cells do not have enough oxygen.

These goals must be addressed concurrently as well as sequentially. That is, you need to focus on them together and recognize that one thing leads to another. Lack of attention to any one goal can result in a domino effect. For example, an anxious patient in severe pain has increased cardiac oxygen demands. If you know this and can lower the demands on the heart by reducing the patient's anxiety and pain, you can slow down the oxygen demand and avoid or reduce the hypoxia, therefore preventing cardiac instability. Unrecognized and/or uncorrected hypoxia promotes cardiac instability, which increases the likelihood of the patient experiencing ventricular fibrillation and loss of circulation. Collectively, these combine to leave you with the challenging and undesirable task of managing a cardiac arrest in the field setting.

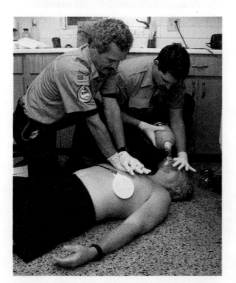

Figure 1-2 Quality patient care is the ultimate goal of every member of the EMS team.

Prevention of Sudden Cardiac Arrest in the Field

Prevention of sudden cardiac arrest in the field setting is one of your most important goals. Few prehospital settings offer ideal circumstances for the management of cardiac arrest. Therefore, your objective is to keep the patient from having sudden cardiac arrest while being transported to the hospital. The hospital, where both personnel and technical resources are plentiful and readily available, offers the best potential for a positive patient outcome.

To prevent sudden cardiac arrest, your interventions need to be focused and fast. When a patient is scared or becomes stressed, the body reacts with a "fight or flight" response, which unleashes a number of chemically active substances into the bloodstream. This causes the heart to beat faster and more forcefully. The increase in cardiac rate and strength of contractions equates with increased cardiac workload. As the workload of the heart increases, so does its need for oxygen to meet increased metabolic demands. If that oxygen need is not met, even briefly, the heart muscle progressively becomes more irritable and susceptible to sudden cardiac arrest. When the patient is in this state, a problem that might be slight in another context can cause sudden cardiac arrest.

Once you have assessed the patient's level of consciousness and identified the chief complaint, try to ease any anxiety quickly while you begin to administer high concentrations of oxygen using a nonrebreathing mask. Being positive yet direct with your comments can help the patient relax. ("Mr. Matthews, please try to relax and take some slow deep breaths. I'm giving you some oxygen, which is going to make you feel better. We are going to take good care of you.") Instill patient confidence by making clear that you are in control of the situation and have a plan of action.

Make the patient as comfortable as possible and discourage unnecessary movement. When the work of the body increases, so does the workload of the heart, thereby increasing the chance of a cardiac arrest. For example, if the patient says "I need to get my coat before I leave," respond by saying "Why don't you stay seated and tell me where it is and what it looks like, and I will get it for you?"

Make certain that the patient's airway is open and breathing and oxygenation are adequate. Decide whether or not you need to call the ALS team to the scene or set up an ALS rendezvous, and prepare the patient for transport. Many definitive cardiac interventions are time sensitive. The sooner you are able to leave the scene, the sooner the patient will arrive at the ALS rendezvous or hospital.

While you wait for the ALS team to arrive, auscultate the patient's breath sounds and obtain a complete set of baseline vital signs. Assess the patient using the OPQRST approach (onset, provoking factors, quality of pain, region and radiation of pain, severity, and time and treatment) presented in Chapter 3. If possible and time permits, obtain a SAMPLE history (signs and symptoms, allergies, medications, past history, last oral intake, and events leading up to the episode). Ask whether the patient has been prescribed medications and, if so, whether they have been taken. Gather all the patient's medications and take them to the hospital. It is important to report baseline information to the incoming ALS team to prevent the same questions from being asked by ALS and hospital personnel. The less overlap there is in patient questioning, the better. Seconds count, and it wastes valuable time to have to repeat the information. Even if the patient is capable of speaking at this point,

Projecting a calm, positive image will reassure the patient and help the call to run more smoothly.

While you wait for the ALS team to arrive, auscultate the patient's breath sounds and obtain a complete set of baseline vital signs.

It is important to report baseline information to the incoming ALS team to prevent the same questions from being asked again.

it is important that oxygen and energy are conserved. By having all the baseline information ready, you will speed up the handoff at each step of the patient's progress to the hospital.

Continually reassess the patient's chief complaint to determine whether the condition has changed and whether anything can be done to make the patient more comfortable. Keep the patient apprised as to what is going on. For example, you could say "The paramedics will be here in just a few minutes. We just spoke with the physicians at the hospital and they are expecting you." Knowing that you have a plan and that it is coming together can reassure your patient, which in turn helps reduce anxiety (**Figure 1-3**).

When the Patient Experiences Sudden Cardiac Arrest

If, despite your best efforts to maintain the patient's physiologic status, your patient collapses while you are on the scene, it is easy to assume the likelihood of sudden cardiac arrest. However, before you act on that assumption, be sure to assess the patient carefully.

The collapse may or may not be sudden cardiac arrest. A patient may lose consciousness because of a rapid drop in blood pressure, caused by cardiac rhythms that are either too fast or too slow. You need to perform all of the steps of a good BLS assessment to be sure you are giving your patient the appropriate care.

That being said, if your patient collapses in front of you, it is time to take action.

1. Confirm the patient's unresponsiveness, open the airway, and check for breathing.
2. If the patient is not breathing, give two rescue breaths and check the carotid pulse. In spite of the hectic moments after a patient collapses, it is important to take at least 5 to 10 seconds to assess the pulse so a weak pulse is not missed.
3. Once you confirm that the patient has no pulse, have your partner begin CPR while you apply an automated external defibrillator (AED) if available and start the analyze mode. AED administration is detailed in Chapter 5.
4. If an AED is not on hand, call for one immediately.
5. When possible, move the patient to a long backboard, which will simplify the move from the floor to the ambulance cot when it is time to transport the patient.

If an AED is readily available, it should be applied immediately and the rhythm analyzed. Studies have shown that up to 85% of victims of nontraumatic sudden cardiac arrest in the prehospital setting initially present in ventricular fibrillation (VF). Other studies place the statistic lower, closer to 60% to 70% (**Figure 1-4**), but in most cases, your patient will be in VF.

When indicated, rapid defibrillation can allow the heart to resume its normal electrical action quickly with a corresponding return of pulse and respirations. Your patient may even regain consciousness.

Figure 1-3 Reassure the patient to help reduce anxiety.

Intervention	Survival Rate
Early defibrillation (6 minutes) with CPR and ALS	30%
Early defibrillation (6 minutes) with CPR	20%
Delayed defibrillation (10 minutes) with CPR	2% to 8%
Delayed defibrillation (10 minutes)	0% to 2%

Adapted from: American Heart Association. *Basic Life Support for Healthcare Providers.* Chandra NC, Hazinski MF, eds. Dallas: American Heart Association; 1997:9-2.

Figure 1-4 Rapid defibrillation can have a profound impact on the likelihood of the patient's survival.

What to Expect When ALS Arrives

Once on scene, the ALS team will reassess the patient. A significant part of that process will include obtaining a hand-off report from the BLS team. Always be sure to provide this report, as skipping it can have far-reaching ramifications. The patient care that has been provided by the BLS team and additional information in the hand-off report are important aspects of the patient care continuum and support a team approach to patient care.

The hand-off report should be brief and to the point. At a minimum, it should include the chief complaint(s). It is also important for the ALS team to know the patient's initial presentation, such as seated on a couch or clutching the chest. Give the information using the OPQRST model to ensure consistency in treatment and reduce the likelihood that you omit something significant. An evaluation of the patient's lung sounds and skin condition, baseline vital signs, and other assessment findings also should be included in your hand-off report. Identify all patient care interventions and the patient's response. Useful information includes such statements as "The patient was complaining of difficulty breathing but stated he had relief from oxygen" or "The patient reported that his chest pain was a 10 on a scale of 1 to 10, and it did not decrease despite administration of 15 L/min of oxygen for 6 minutes via a nonrebreathing mask." Valuable information is not necessarily good news. The ALS team must quickly ascertain which interventions have been performed and whether or not a difference was made in the patient's condition. Once the hand-off report has been completed and is given to an ALS provider, the ALS team assumes responsibility for patient care (**Figure 1-5**).

It is critical that the transition of care from BLS to ALS providers be as smooth as possible. For some BLS providers, making the change from running the call to being in a primary support role is difficult. A good way to facilitate the transition after completion of the hand-off report is to ask the ALS provider "What else would you like us to do?" This makes it clear that you have handed off and that the patient is now the responsibility of the ALS team. It shows that you are ready for them to

Completion of the hand-off report by BLS personnel and review by ALS personnel are steps that should never be skipped.

Figure 1-5 The hand-off report is an important aspect of the patient care continuum.

direct you in how you can assist them with the patient's care in the required capacity.

While one ALS team member is taking the hand-off report, another will be initiating additional patient care measures. If the patient is not on a cardiac monitor, the paramedic will apply the quick-look paddles to see whether the patient is in a shockable rhythm. If the need for a shock is confirmed, the paramedic will prepare to shock the patient per local protocol. In the case where defibrillation is indicated, the initial series (up to three shocks) can take up to a minute or longer. It is crucial that other members of the team make good use of this time. As the EMT-B on hand, you may be directed to prepare intubation supplies while the other ALS team member is oxygenating the patient with a bag-valve-mask (BVM) device and 100% oxygen. You may be assigned equipment preparation and the preoxygenation of the patient while an ALS team member is trying to obtain IV access. These procedures are discussed in detail in Chapter 2.

If the patient is on a cardiac monitor when the ALS team arrives, electrodes may need to be changed or added so the paramedics can switch the patient over to their own monitor/defibrillator.

Another possible plan of action may be to initiate patient transport immediately and provide additional patient care en route to the hospital. In this case, you will need to gather up any equipment, prepare the cot, and make certain that the way to exit the emergency scene is clear.

In some EMS systems, if a patient has not been resuscitated after defibrillation, intubation, and reasonable efforts at drug therapy, the decision to stop resuscitative efforts may be made by medical control. In that case, it may be necessary to contact the medical examiner or a funeral home. Check your local protocols for direction with regard to what EMS personnel should do in the event of patient death. In this situation, make certain that family members or responsible parties are notified of the patient's death. Survivors on the scene will need gentle, caring support from the EMS team.

By working well together, the BLS and ALS team members can improve the quality of care being rendered as well as the efficiency with which the care is provided.

Wrap Up

**Chapter 1
The EMT-B and the Advanced Life
Support Team**

Ready for Review

This chapter has described cardiac arrest, the importance of basic life support in cardiac cases, the working relationship between BLS and ALS providers, and the importance of a hand-off report. It also has introduced the benefit of the ALS rendezvous or tiered response in improved outcomes for patients experiencing cardiac arrest in the prehospital setting.

Quick Case

1. Your squad is dispatched to a man "feeling ill" at an extended care facility. On arrival, you find that your patient is in full cardia carrest. You initiate CPR and prepare to apply the AED when the charge nurse tells you she thinks the downtime on this patient was most likely between 5 and 8 minutes before 9-1-1 was called.

   Assuming that the nurse's time estimate is reliable, how would this extended downtime impact the likelihood of the patient being successfully resuscitated?

   _____

   _____

2. A response to a local restaurant for an "unknown medical" finds you caring for a 59-year-old man with crushing chest pain and difficulty breathing. Onset of symptoms was approximately 1 hour prior, and the patient received no relief from taking two of his nitroglycerin tablets. He has been treated for angina for the last 2 years but has never had an experience like this.

   What are the five main principles of care for all patients with cardiac emergencies?

   _____

   _____

3. You are transporting a 70-year-old female patient to the emergency department for a complaint of abdominal pain. While you are obtaining a baseline blood pressure, the patient suddenly gasps and slumps forward in full cardiac arrest.

   As you initiate care for this patient, what should you recall as being the two main goals of cardiac arrest management in the prehospital setting?

   _____

   _____

   _____

Chapter 2

Airway Evaluation and Control

The importance of maintaining a patent airway and ensuring adequacy of breathing cannot be overstated in patients being managed in the prehospital setting. This is even more critical for emergent patients with problems of cardiac origin.

You also must understand that airway care is more than a one-time check. Evaluating and controlling the airway and breathing are ongoing processes that require your constant attention throughout the time the patient is in your care.

Of all the muscles in the body, the heart is one of the least tolerant of even brief interruptions in its oxygen flow. When a patient is in a cardiac-related crisis, the heart works harder. Patients are typically anxious and/or frightened and, as the crisis continues, become even more so. At some point, the fight-or-flight response kicks in as a result of the actions of the **sympathetic nervous system**, and cardiac work increases markedly.

Depending on the nature of the cardiac crisis, whether it is angina or an actual heart attack, the heart works harder to compensate for the decreased oxygen supply. No matter what the precipitating event, with any increase in cardiac workload comes a corresponding increase in cardiac oxygen demand. If this demand for oxygen is not met, tissue and blood oxygen levels decrease and the heart becomes more ischemic, making it more irritable and electrically unstable. If this oxygen inadequacy continues, there may be increased cardiac irritability, which makes the heart more likely to fibrillate. Once ventricular fibrillation occurs, there is an immediate loss of effective pumping action and the patient goes into cardiac arrest.

Airway evaluation and control is the dynamic, almost circular process of evaluating, managing, and reevaluating the patient to make certain that the airway remains patent and breathing is adequate.

The effective evaluation and control of your patient's overall respiratory status can be broken down into three distinct yet related components:

- Anatomic
- Mechanical
- Chemical

Understanding how these three key components of respiration relate to each other will help you to control them effectively.

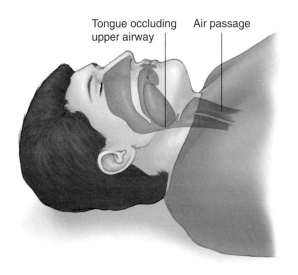

Figure 2-1 In an unconscious patient, loss of muscle tone allows the tongue to fall into the throat and block the airway.

Anatomic Issues

Foremost, the anatomic structures of the airway must be open and patent, because it is the conduit through which oxygen-rich air from the outside environment passes into the lungs. Without unobstructed and properly positioned anatomy, there is no possibility of adequate inflow and outflow of air. Anatomic positioning is the foundation on which airway evaluation and control are built.

As a rule, conscious, alert, and spontaneously breathing patients are capable of protecting their own airway. Even a small piece of food falling upon the epiglottis will stimulate a cough as the body instantly responds to keep the foreign body out of the airway. However, when patients lose consciousness, their airway protection capabilities become impaired. Loss of muscle tone allows the tongue to fall backward into the pharynx, which in turn can produce a variety of consequences ranging from snoring respirations to complete obstruction of the airway (**Figure 2-1**).

In the absence of trauma, the most common technique for opening the airway is the **head tilt-chin lift maneuver** (**Figure 2-2**). For an unconscious trauma patient with a suspected neck injury, the **jaw-thrust maneuver** is considered to best spare the spine from further injury, as it can be performed without tilting the head back (**Skill Drill 2-1**). However, should either the head tilt-chin lift or jaw-thrust prove unsuccessful in producing an open airway, the head should be tilted back slowly until the airway is open and patent.

Positioning techniques should be used first when attempting to open an obstructed airway because they can be employed quickly without any equipment. It would not be efficient to have to search for a piece of equipment, when a minute or two could make the difference in whether or not the patient goes into respiratory or possibly even cardiac arrest.

sympathetic nervous system
The part of the autonomic nervous system responsible for defensive, compensatory responses; often called the fight-or-flight system.

head tilt-chin lift maneuver
A combination of two movements to open the airway by tilting the forehead back and lifting the chin; used for non-trauma patients.

jaw-thrust maneuver
Technique to open the airway by placing the fingers behind the angle of the jaw and bringing the jaw forward; used when a patient may have a cervical spine injury.

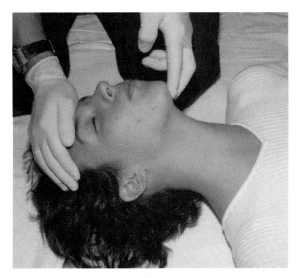

Figure 2-2 The head tilt-chin lift maneuver is a simple technique for opening the airway in a patient without a suspected cervical spine injury.

SkillDrill 2-1 Performing a Jaw-Thrust Maneuver

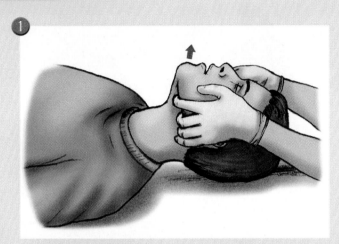

1

Kneeling above the patient's head, place your fingers behind the angles of the lower jaw, and forcefully move the jaw upward. Use your thumbs to help position the lower jaw.

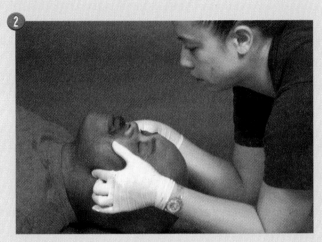

2

The completed maneuver should look like this.

Positioning techniques should be used first when attempting to open an obstructed airway because they can be employed quickly without any equipment.

Figure 2-3 Suction any fluid or particles from the mouth before any attempt to intubate.

For spontaneously breathing patients, simply correcting the position of the head, neck, and mandible may be all that is required to reestablish a patent airway. However, once that is accomplished, an airway adjunct such as an oropharyngeal or nasopharyngeal airway may be necessary to maintain airway patency in cases where patients are unable to do so on their own.

The use of suction also may be needed for controlling airway patency. Complete airway obstruction can result when a patient's posterior pharynx is full of blood or vomit. To make matters worse, a situation such as this greatly increases the likelihood of aspiration, which is associated with short- and long-term implications. In the short term, airway obstruction and the corresponding loss of oxygen inflow are of primary concern. In the long term, patients who may be fortunate enough to survive but have aspirated blood or stomach contents into their lungs may now have to deal with aspiration pneumonia and/or adult respiratory distress syndrome (ARDS). Either condition increases patient morbidity or mortality.

As an alert EMT-B, you should be quick to recognize the need for suction and always have the equipment set up. This preparation includes being sure that whatever suction device is to be used has a catheter in place and is capable of removing large materials, such as blood clots or food chunks (**Figure 2-3**). Measure the catheter from the corner of the mouth to the earlobe and follow the steps in **Skill Drill 2-2**. The posterior pharynx is far more frequently in need of suction than is the tracheobronchial tree, so it would be wise to keep a larger size tip catheter in place as a first-line suction tool. Whistle-tip catheters are not advised as a first-line suction tool. Although useful for the tracheobronchial tree, they are useless if clots are present or partially digested food is regurgi-

SkillDrill 2-2 Suctioning a Patient's Airway

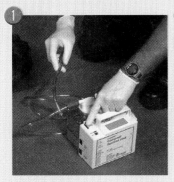

1. Make sure the suctioning unit is properly assembled and turn on the suction unit.

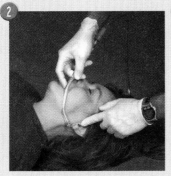

2. Measure the catheter from the corner of the mouth to the earlobe.

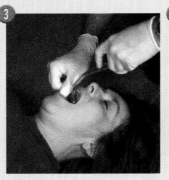

3. Open the patient's mouth and insert the catheter to the depth measured.

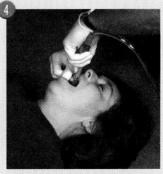

4. Apply suction in a circular motion as you withdraw the catheter. Do not suction an adult for more than 15 seconds.

tated. By keeping one of the larger tips on your suction tube, you can avoid wasting time changing catheters, since those few seconds may be all the time it takes for your patient to aspirate the material or for the airway to become totally obstructed.

Finally, it is important to keep in mind a common and serious complication of suctioning—the possibility of producing moderate to severe hypoxemia in your patient. As you are suctioning foreign secretions, you are also vacuuming out whatever residual oxygen supply might have been in the patient's airways and lungs. This inadvertent removal of oxygen can result in cerebral and cardiac ischemia, which in turn can cause cardiac rhythm changes and possibly even precipitate sudden cardiac arrest. To avoid this complication, limit suction to no more than 10 seconds in adults and 5 seconds in children.

Mechanical Considerations

The process of breathing is a combination of two different mechanical events: inspiration and expiration. During inspiration, the normally dome-shaped diaphragm flattens and the muscles of the upper thorax expand, increasing the size of the chest cavity. These actions combine to create a negative intrathoracic pressure, causing air to be drawn into the lungs. During expiration, the muscles of the upper thorax relax, and the chest wall returns to its normal position. At the same time, the diaphragm returns to its normal dome-like shape. Therefore, inspiration is considered to be an *active process* when compared to the usually *passive process* of expiration.

Each cycle of inspiration and expiration produces a single breath. Effective evaluation of breathing involves more than just counting breaths per minute and comparing that number to the normal baseline standard

Table 2-1: Normal Respiration Rate Ranges

Adults	12 to 20 breaths/min
Children	15 to 30 breaths/min
Infants	25 to 50 breaths/min

Rate × Depth = Minute Volume

of 12 to 20 breaths/min for adults (**Table 2-1**). In truth, your assessment needs to consider the rate of breathing as well as the depth of each breath. A patient breathing at a rate of 10 breaths/min and taking slow, deep breaths may be exchanging oxygen and carbon dioxide efficiently. By comparison, a patient breathing at a rate of 18 breaths/min and taking shallow breaths may be in serious respiratory distress. Multiplying the respiratory rate times depth of respirations (in mL) results in what is called minute volume. For the average adult patient, minute volume usually is about 6,000 mL. Minute volumes of approximately 1,500 mL with a corresponding respiratory rate of between 2 and 4 breaths/min will only sustain life for several minutes unless there is pronounced slowing of metabolism, which could be the case in severe hypothermia.

Evaluating the Adequacy of Breathing

The following steps should be taken to evaluate the adequacy of breathing:

- **Look at your patient's skin color**—A blue or gray tint usually indicates oxygen desaturation. Keep in mind that darker-skinned people often will first show signs of cyanosis in areas such as their nail beds, the sclera of the eye, around the lips, and/or the inner mucosa of their lips.

- **Assess the work of breathing**—Breathing usually is an automatic, effortless process that requires no thought or exertion. If a patient appears to be working hard at breathing, assume that there is a problem. Take immediate steps to identify and address the problem by assisting the patient's respiratory efforts with a bag-valve-mask (BVM) device hooked up to high-flow oxygen. Observe for accessory muscle use, retractions, and inability to speak in full sentences, ie, one- or two-word dyspnea.

- **Listen to your patient's breathing**—The age-old maxim "Loud breathing is bad breathing" remains true today. Wet, gurgling sounds in the upper airway represent a potential life threat because of interference with air inflow. Wheezing or whistling breath sounds may indicate reduced airflow through the smaller airways in the lungs, which can indicate a reduction of oxygen reaching the **alveoli**.

alveoli
The air sacs of the lungs in which the exchange of oxygen and carbon dioxide takes place.

Chemical Processes/Gas Exchange

Open, patent anatomy and adequate mechanical activity lead to the third component of respiration—the chemical process of gas exchange. With each inhaled breath comes another batch of oxygen-laden air, while each exhaled breath removes carbon dioxide, one of the principal waste products of metabolism. This process must continue uninterrupted for the body to maintain a pH and acid–base balance that is within the acceptable limits for biologic functions to continue. A patient's acid–base balance is reported as a blood pH, with a pH of 7.35 to 7.45 considered normal and a pH of 6.9 and 7.8 considered the extreme limits at which life can exist (**Figure 2-4**). When gas exchange does not occur in a section of lung, for example because of pulmonary edema, a potentially lethal series of events begins. In this situation, blood containing high levels of carbon dioxide (CO_2) returns to the systemic circulation still loaded with CO_2

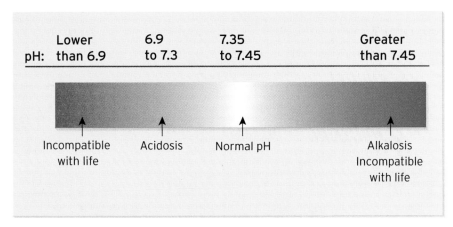

pH:	Lower than 6.9	6.9 to 7.3	7.35 to 7.45	Greater than 7.45

Incompatible with life   Acidosis   Normal pH   Alkalosis Incompatible with life

Figure 2-4 pH scale: acidosis, normal, and alkalosis.

rather than with oxygen. The relationship between carbon dioxide and pH is inverse. The body perceives carbon dioxide as an acid. Therefore, as CO_2 levels rise, the pH falls. When the pH continues to fall, the body becomes increasingly acidotic, causing the heart to function less effectively. In addition, overall cellular function becomes less efficient.

Although it is true that the body has alternative means of meeting its metabolic needs, because these means are less efficient, they produce not only more metabolic waste, but also more *toxic* metabolic waste.

One of the most significant contributions you can make as an EMT-B within ACLS and emergency cardiac care is in airway evaluation and control. You should be constantly monitoring anatomic positioning and making certain that a patent airway *stays patent*. The importance of having suction ready has already been stated. It is common to find an EMT-B using a BVM device to ventilate an intubated patient. Any of these functions, all of which you can perform as an EMT-B, can free up ALS providers to focus on skills that they alone must perform. In the end, it all adds up to improved patient care.

Primary Adjuncts for Airway Control

Just as prehospital medicine has evolved, so has the potpourri of mechanical devices known as airway adjuncts. There are many choices to be made as you attempt to improve the ventilation and oxygenation of your patient.

Oropharyngeal Airways

The oropharyngeal (oral) airway is a curved device, usually made of plastic, designed to hold the tongue off the posterior aspect of the pharynx (**Figure 2-5**). It is only used in unconscious patients, because it may stimulate gagging, vomiting, and possibly even laryngospasm in the conscious or semiconscious patient. Oropharyngeal airways are easily placed and when in position serve to facilitate suctioning. They also may be used to prevent intubated patients from chewing or biting on the endotracheal tube.

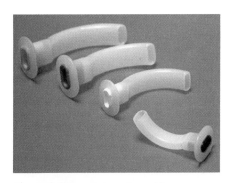

Figure 2-5 An oral airway is used for unconscious patients who have no gag reflex. It keeps the tongue from blocking the airway and makes suctioning the airway easier.

Skill Drill 2-3 Inserting an Oral Airway

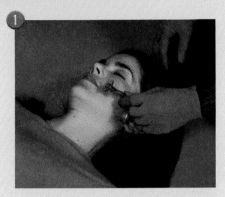

Size the airway by measuring from the patient's earlobe to the corner of the mouth.

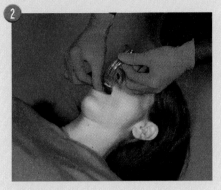

Open the patient's mouth with the cross-finger technique. Hold the airway upside down with your other hand. Insert the airway with the tip facing the roof of the mouth.

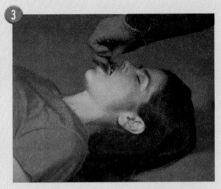

Rotate the airway 180°. Insert the airway until the flange (the trumpet-shaped flare) rests on the patient's lips and teeth. In this position, the airway will hold the tongue forward.

Placing the correct size oropharyngeal airway is essential because one that is too large or too small will not function properly and may compromise the airway. The oropharyngeal airway is sized by measuring the distance from the corner of the patient's mouth to the angle of the mandible (earlobe) and comparing that to the distance from the flange to the distal tip of the oropharyngeal airway.

When trauma is not a factor, the oropharyngeal airway is placed by tilting the patient's head back and turning the device in a curve-up position (**Skill Drill 2-3**). After insertion has begun, and as the distal tip nears the posterior pharnyx, it should be rotated, allowing the curve of the device to follow the natural curve of the tongue. Placement is confirmed by closing the nostrils and listening for clear and equal breath sounds during ventilation. Any time an oropharyngeal airway is being used, the patient's head must continue to be tilted back.

Nasopharyngeal Airways

Unlike the oropharyngeal airway, which is only used in unconscious, unresponsive patients, the nasopharyngeal airway can be placed in semi-conscious patients (**Figure 2-6**). Ample lubrication prior to insertion reduces the likelihood of damaging the nasal mucosa and causing unnecessary bleeding usually accompanied by injuries of this type.

A nasopharyngeal airway is a tubular device made of flexible rubber or plastic that usually is used when an oropharyngeal airway is too difficult to place or cannot be placed, such as when the patient has a gag reflex. Trismus (clenched teeth), extensive facial trauma, the presence of the gag reflex, or bleeding into the posterior pharynx that requires extensive suctioning are some examples of when a nasopharyngeal airway might be a better choice of airway adjuncts.

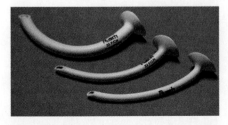

Figure 2-6 A nasal airway is better tolerated by patients who have an intact gag reflex.

Skill Drill 2-4   Inserting a Nasal Airway

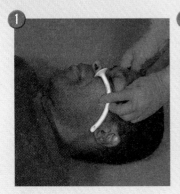

1 Size the airway by measuring from the tip of the nose to the patient's earlobe. Coat the tip with a water-soluble lubricant.

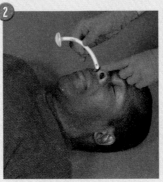

2 Insert the lubricated airway into the larger nostril with the curvature following the floor of the nose and the bevel toward the septum.

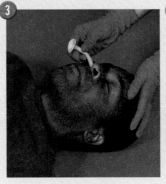

3 Gently advance the airway.

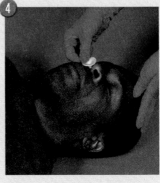

4 Continue until the flange rests against the skin. If you feel any resistance or obstruction, remove the airway and insert it into the other nostril.

The nasopharyngeal airway is sized according to the internal diameter of the tube. As the diameter of the tube increases there also is a proportional increase in the length of the tube. Guidelines for size selections are as follows:

- Large adult—8.0 to 9.0 mm
- Medium adult—7.0 to 8.0 mm
- Small adult—6.0 to 7.0 mm

The EMT-B can select the right size nasopharyngeal airway as well as prepare and place it, allowing the paramedic to perform other critical tasks. Size the nasopharyngeal airway by measuring from the tip of the nose to the patient's earlobe. As with the oropharyngeal airway, proper sizing is an important concern. If the nasopharyngeal airway is too long, it could extend partially into the esophagus. This should be suspected if you notice gastric distension or hypoventilation during ventilations, in which case the nasopharyngeal airway should be removed and replaced with the next smaller size.

Lung sounds and the overall quality of ventilations should be reassessed after replacing the nasopharyngeal airway. Observe for gagging, vomiting, and laryngospasms when using a nasopharyngeal airway on a responsive patient. Finally, be sure that proper anatomic position is maintained whenever using a nasopharyngeal airway by use of the head tilt-chin lift method. In the case of a trauma patient, use of the jaw-thrust maneuver is preferred for maintaining proper anatomic position.

Prior to insertion, the nasopharyngeal airway should be well lubricated with a water-soluble lubricant. In some cases, the lubricant may include an anesthetic agent. The nasopharyngeal airway should be inserted gently, with even more care being required if it is made of plastic, because the rubber nasopharyngeal airways tend to be softer and more forgiving of the nasal mucosa (**Skill Drill 2-4**). The end of the nasopharyngeal airway is cut at a soft angle, and it can be rotated slightly if resistance is encountered during insertion.

Endotracheal Intubation

In the world of airway control, the endotracheal (ET) tube remains the gold standard. When a properly sized ET tube is placed and the cuff on the distal end is inflated, it isolates the airway completely, providing increased protection from aspiration of blood or gastric contents. In addition, the ET tube can also be used to deliver close to 100% oxygen, while allowing direct access for suctioning of the tracheobronchial tree. In cases where IV access is difficult or impossible to obtain, as in a cardiac arrest, the ET tube also can serve as an alternate route for administering a limited selection of drugs.

Placing an ET tube can range in difficulty from moderate to impossible, depending on certain variables, including anatomic features of the patient, the physical condition of the patient, and the circumstances under which the ET tube must be placed. Good hand-eye coordination, proper preparation, and good technique are the keys to a successful intubation. An EMT-B who is well versed in this area can be a valuable asset.

The technology involved with intubation is not complex. The laryngoscope is little more than a handle to which the laryngoscope blade is attached. The handle also serves as the place where the batteries used to illuminate the light source are kept.

Laryngoscope blades come in a variety of sizes and shapes that quickly snap on to the handle at a 90° angle. Each blade has either a tiny removable bulb or fiber optics at the distal end that serves to illuminate the key anatomic landmarks guiding the intubation.

The two basic choices of blades are straight (Miller) (**Figure 2-7**) or curved (Macintosh) (**Figure 2-8**). There are several minor variations of each, but these are the two main types.

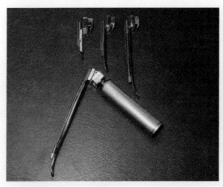

Figure 2-7 Miller blades.

Figure 2-8 Macintosh blades.

Prior to attempting to intubate a patient, a number of activities need to occur: assembling the necessary equipment and preoxygenating the patient, because no ventilations can occur during the intubation process. Ideally, all should occur simultaneously, to further expedite the process of securing the airway. This preparatory phase of the intubation is where you can play a key role. Usually, the person performing the intubation assembles and checks the equipment, while another member of the EMS team positions and preoxygenates the patient. Depending on other aspects of patient care underway, you might find yourself responsible for both stages of the preparation. Therefore, it is beneficial to be knowledgeable of the entire process.

Preparing the Patient

All adult patients should be positioned with the head elevated to enhance alignment of the anatomic axes. In some cases, placing a folded towel under the occiput can further assist with positioning.

Insert an oral airway and preoxygenate the patient for 1 to 2 minutes with 100% oxygen with a BVM device. If a pulse oximeter is available, apply it so that the intubation can proceed once the saturation is at 100% (**Figure 2-9**). This helps to ensure that the body has a good residual supply of oxygen to draw upon during the 20 to 30 seconds often required to place the ET tube, during which time no ventilations can occur.

There are a number of impediments to using a BVM device effectively, including beards and mustaches, facial fractures, displaced or misplaced dentures, obesity, and upper airway obstructions. The most common impediment, however, is poor technique on the part of the BVM operator.

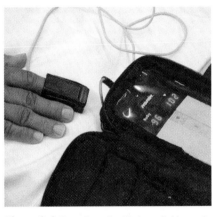

Figure 2-9 If a pulse oximeter is available, apply it so that the intubation can proceed once the saturation is at 100%.

For cardiac arrest patients who are obviously apneic, there is almost a 100% certainty that they have elevated CO_2 levels. Ventilating patients at a slightly faster rate than normal during the preoxygenation phase may help to decrease their CO_2 levels. It is crucial to remember that they will not be ventilated during the intubation attempt, and you should expect their CO_2 levels to increase slowly until such time as ventilations resume. Ideally, a capnometer should be used to monitor the CO_2 level, which is normally in the range of approximately 40 mm Hg (**Figure 2-10**). You should be cautious not to hyperventilate patients excessively because of the vasoconstrictive effects of decreased CO_2. Carbon dioxide levels of less than 25 mm Hg can result in severe cerebral hypoxia.

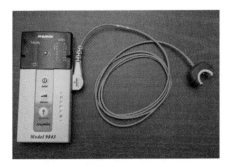

Figure 2-10 Ideally, a capnometer should be used to monitor the CO_2 level.

Preparing the Equipment

The correct style and size of laryngoscope blade should be selected based on the patient's age, anatomy, and size. Children younger than 8 years usually require a straight blade. The flange on the Macintosh blade helps control the tongue more easily than does a Miller. Most seasoned ALS providers have developed a preference for one style or another. If providers don't make their preference known, don't hesitate to ask.

The notched area on the proximal end of the blade slides over the round bar on the top of the laryngoscope handle. Snap the two together to engage. As the blade is lifted up, it pivots on the bar and locks into place at a 90° angle. The light should illuminate when properly assembled. For blades with a removable bulb, the bulb should be checked to be sure it is *tight, white, and bright,* or securely screwed in place and giving off a bright white light, which is your indication that there is ample power in the batteries. A dimly lit bulb indicates a potentially failing power source, in which case a different handle should be chosen or the batteries changed quickly lest the light fail during intubation.

Next, select the correct size ET tube. As with all airways, ET tubes come in a variety of sizes based on the internal diameter of the tube (measured in millimeters) (**Figure 2-11**). Often, the person performing the intubation will request the size believed to be most appropriate based on the size of the patient's nostril or little finger. Prepare one size smaller and one larger than requested as well. Also, take note of the horizontal marks placed at intervals down the length of the tube. These serve as reference points to gauge the depth of tube placement. When the tube is pushed to the corner of the mouth, the mark on the tube closest to that anatomic point should be identified. For an adult man, expect the tube to be at 21 to 23 cm, or 19 to 21 cm for an adult woman. These are only guidelines. Variations in neck length/jaw structure can alter anticipated depth levels, though they should not be markedly different. Once tube placement has been confirmed, a periodic glance at your reference mark will help to ensure that the tube has not been pushed farther down into the trachea or possibly pulled out.

Average ET tubes usually are 7.0 to 8.0 mm for an adult woman and 8.0 to 8.5 mm for an adult man. All adult size ET tubes are made of semi-rigid plastic with a 15-mm adapter on the proximal end. The adapter fits a variety of devices used to provide positive pressure ventilation (**Figure 2-12**). ET tubes used on adult patients have a high-volume, low-pressure cuff near the distal end of the tube that is inflated after the tube is positioned. This is designed to seal the space that remains around the tube and to prevent air leaks during ventilations. It also reduces the risk of blood, vomit, or secretions making their way down the airway and being aspirated into the lungs. Attach a 10-mL syringe to the one-way valve, and insert about 8 to 10 mL of air to confirm that the cuff works and is not leaking. Assuming all is well, withdraw the air, at which time the cuff should deflate completely and collapse around the ET tube.

Whenever the cuff on an ET tube is inflated, the pilot bulb or balloon next to the one-way valve also will inflate. As long as the cuff remains inflated, the pilot bulb should remain firm. If the pilot bulb deflates, this signals that the cuff has failed and that the airway is no longer protected

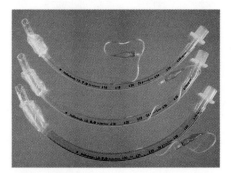

Figure 2-11 Endotracheal tubes that are used on adults generally range in size from 7.0 to 8.5 mm. Note the centimeter markings.

Figure 2-12 The components of the adult endotracheal tube include a 15-mm adapter that attaches to a ventilating device, a pilot balloon, the tube, a balloon cuff (shown inflated), and the Murphy eye. The pediatric tube shown at the bottom includes an adapter and a Murphy eye at the uncuffed distal end of the tube.

from aspiration. Should you notice this, *immediately* let the paramedic or ALS provider in charge of patient care know what has happened and take action.

After the laryngoscope handle and blade have been selected and checked, and the ET cuff has been checked, assemble the following remaining equipment:

- Stylet for inserting the ET tube
- Water-soluble lubricant
- Suction unit with large-bore tonsil tip in place
- Magill forceps for foreign body removal/aid to tube placement
- Esophageal intubation detector devices (EIDD), capnoflow or capnometer unit, or end-tidal CO_2 detector (colormetric device)
- Stethoscope
- Bite block, or oropharyngeal airway
- Tape

Intubating the Patient

Once the patient is preoxygenated and all the equipment is ready, it is time to begin the intubation. In most cases, the EMT-B continues ventilating with the BVM device until the intubator signals to stop ventilations. At that time, the oropharyngeal airway is removed. The patient's head is gently lifted and placed into the "sniffing" position, meaning that the neck is flexed and the head is slightly elevated. Again, a small rolled up or folded towel may be placed behind the patient's head to achieve the desired posture. The purpose of this positioning is to realign the close-to-90° angle of the mouth, pharynx, and trachea to allow for better visualization of the vocal cords.

Patients intubated in the operating room setting are medicated, have empty stomachs, and are anatomically dry. None of these three hospital environment conveniences usually apply to field intubations. As soon as ventilations cease, the laryngoscope is held in the intubator's left hand and gently inserted into the mouth from the right side, sweeping the tongue to the left, and moved into position in order to visualize the landmarks of the airway (**Figure 2-13**). Just prior to insertion, you or another EMT-B can lubricate the tube with water-soluble jelly to facilitate a smooth pass of the tube and to help minimize damage to sensitive tissues, such as the vocal cords.

The tongue is swept to the left and as the blade reaches midline, it is advanced toward the posterior pharynx. Be prepared to suction or to hand the intubator the suction if the situation warrants. If a straight blade is being used, the epiglottis is lifted directly. By comparison, if a curved blade is being used, the distal tip is inserted into the valeculla (the area between the base of the tongue and the epiglottis), and the epiglottis is lifted indirectly (**Figure 2-14**). The EMT-B may be asked to depress the cricoid cartilage (Sellick maneuver) (**Figure 2-15**). This is accomplished by placing two fingers over the cricoid membrane (Adam's

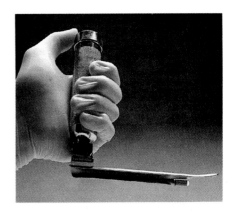

Figure 2-13 The laryngoscope is held in the left hand, and the blade is inserted in the right side of the mouth.

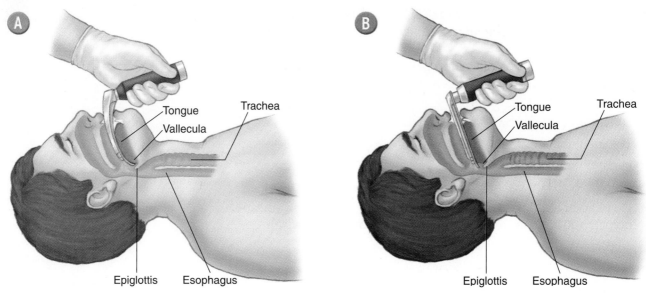

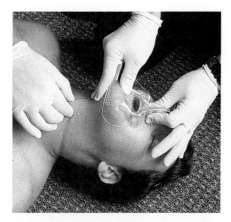

Figure 2-14 A. Insert a curved blade just in front of the epiglottis into the vallecula. **B.** Insert a straight blade past the epiglottis.

Figure 2-15 The Sellick maneuver is performed by depressing the cricoid cartilage approximately $1/2$" with two fingers.

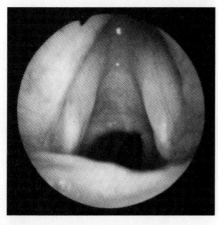

Figure 2-16 A view of the vocal cords.

apple) and gently pushing down to a depth of approximately $1/2$". This technique serves a dual purpose because it helps partially occlude the esophagus, which in turn helps prevent aspiration, should vomiting occur. At the same time, it improves the visualization process by bringing the trachea and the surrounding structures into view.

The glottic opening and the vocal cords should now come into view (**Figure 2-16**). These are the key landmarks during an intubation. Without clear visualization of the cords, the insertion of an ET tube is termed a "blind intubation" and almost without fail will result in the tube passing into the esophagus rather than the trachea.

After visualizing the key landmarks, the tube is inserted and *must* be seen passing through the vocal cords. The laryngoscope is gently removed from the patient's mouth, avoiding any contact with the teeth or lips. If a stylet was used, it is removed at this time. At this point, look for the mark on the ET tube in reference to the edge of the patient's mouth. The cuff will be inflated and the syringe removed, during which time the EMT-B should reattach the BVM device and begin to ventilate the patient. Expect to provide at least three ventilations, so that equal breath sounds over each lung can be confirmed as well as the absence of sounds over the epigastrium. Do not overinflate the lungs. Allow time for exhalation. Recheck breath sounds after cuff inflation. Nothing should be heard over the stomach other than normal gastric sounds. Bubbling or gurgling over the stomach, absence of chest wall movement, and absence of breath sounds point to an esophageal intubation.

If the esophagus has been inadvertently intubated, reattach the syringe, deflate the cuff, and remove the tube. Ventilate the patient for 20 to 30 seconds or until the pulse oximeter again shows 100% saturation. Remember that it is not unusual to intubate the esophagus, but it is unacceptable to not recognize the situation and leave the ET tube improperly placed! An unrecognized esophageal tube still works to isolate the lungs. However, in this case no oxygen will enter the lungs, and after 4 to 6 minutes, permanent brain damage is certain.

Correct tube placement can be confirmed even further using a capnometer, some form of an end-tidal CO_2 detector, or esophageal intubation detector device (EIDD). When correct placement has been confirmed, secure the ET tube by using tape or one of a variety of commercially available devices. In some systems, an oropharyngeal airway is placed beside the ET tube to serve as a bite block should the patient begin to breathe on his or her own. Breath sounds should be checked again as well as the reference mark on the side of the tube next to the corner of the patient's mouth. As the EMT-B continues to ventilate the patient, the mark should be checked periodically to make certain the tube has not become misplaced (pulled out or slipped down). If the ET tube has been pushed down, it will usually enter the right mainstem bronchus. This is confirmed if breath sounds are present on the right side and absent or diminished on the left side or if oxygen saturation levels begin to fall on the pulse oximeter. Should this occur, the quick fix is to deflate the cuff partially and gently pull the tube back about $1/2$", while simultaneously ventilating and rechecking breath sounds. If bilateral breath sounds reappear, the cuff should be reinflated, the tube resecured, and ventilations resumed. Occasionally, the tube may be withdrawn too far and come out of the trachea. This is undesirable because it requires restarting the whole intubation process. In many cases, a repeat intubation is harder than the first, so inadvertent extubation should be avoided.

The actual intubation—from cessation of ventilations to giving the first breath to confirming proper placement—should not take any more than 30 seconds; 15 to 20 seconds is preferable. If 30 seconds pass during an intubation attempt, be prepared to replace the oropharyngeal airway and ventilate the patient for a minimum of 15 to 30 seconds or until 100% saturation is again reached. At that time, the oropharyngeal airway can be removed and another attempt made.

As long as the respiratory or cardiac arrest continues, the patient should be ventilated with about 700 to 800 mL of oxygen at 15 to 20 breaths/min. For obese patients, increase the volume slightly while reducing it slightly for smaller adults. When the patient is resuscitated, the ventilation rate can be slowed down to 12 to 16 breaths/min.

With proper technique and ideal circumstances, endotracheal intubation can be almost without complication. However, complications do occur and can include lacerations of the lip or tongue, chipped teeth, soft-tissue damage, and tracheal swelling or bleeding. The most common reasons for failure to intubate are inadequate equipment preparation and/or incorrect patient positioning, *which occur prior to actually using the laryngoscope.*

> **R**emember that it is not unusual to intubate the esophagus, but it is unacceptable to not recognize the situation and leave the ET tube improperly placed!

Wrap Up

Chapter 2
Airway Evaluation and Control

Ready for Review

This chapter has presented step-by-step instruction on how to evaluate the state of patient airways and how to remove blockages. The head tilt-chin lift and jaw-thrust maneuvers are described as methods for opening the airway. The correct preparation and use of suction equipment is presented. You now know why airway management is essential in order for the lungs to continue to perform the chemical processes and gas exchange tasks essential to life. In addition, you have seen how to intubate patients through both the oropharyngeal and nasopharyngeal airways. You have become familiar with the Sellick maneuver and clearly understand the need for smooth teamwork of both BLS and ALS to improve the chances of survival for your cardiac patient.

Quick Case

1.) A man collapses at a high school football game and is found to be in full arrest. He is shocked three times without converting, and CPR continues as you await the arrival of ALS. Once on scene, the paramedic is preparing to intubate and asks you to hyperventilate and hyperoxygenate the patient for 2 minutes as he prepares his equipment.

What is the purpose of this?

_____

_____

2.) You respond to the local YMCA where you find an 80-year-old man unconscious and unresponsive in the dining hall. As you approach, you see that his head is slumped forward on his chest and that he is extremely cyanotic.

What does the patient's skin color imply? How should you initially manage this patient's airway problem?

_____

_____

3.) EMS is called to a private residence and arrives to find a 62-year-old man in acute respiratory distress. The patient has a long cardiac history. His wife tells you that he may have accidentally taken too many painkillers given to him for a recent foot surgery. You notice that the patient appears to be breathing approximately 6 times a minute and the breaths are shallow.

How can this respiratory situation adversely impact this patient's cardiac condition? What is your initial focus relative to this patient's respiratory status?

_____

_____

_____

From Angina to AMI: The Cardiac Care Continuum

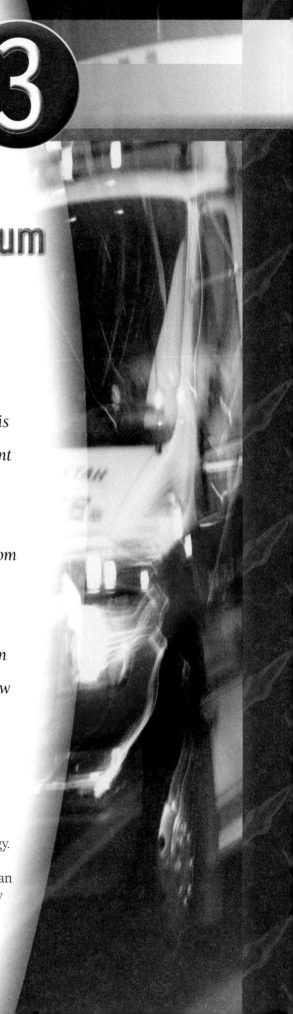

I n recent years, there has been a move to teach EMT-Bs assessment-based, or what might be better termed "complaint-based" medicine. As with most ideas, this is not without its pros and cons. Proponents of this movement argue that an EMT-B has neither the depth nor breadth of knowledge base to facilitate doing a differential diagnosis, nor is that appropriate or necessary at this level of care. From a practical perspective, there is no difference in the EMT-B care that is rendered to a patient having an angina attack when compared to the care provided to the patient having an AMI. However, it is the goal of this text to teach EMT-Bs how to better care for patients with cardiac-related problems, so that their contributions to the team are increased.

There is a distinct drawback when attempting to use a complaint-based approach: The patient generally will not use medical terminology. Although "chest pain" may be the chief complaint expected by a field provider, ischemia may manifest itself in many different ways other than chest pain. In addition, basing patient care on the assumption that any given patient will use accurate, recognizable medical terminology and descriptions is not realistic or practical. Therefore, having excellent patient assessment skills and then cultivating the ability to *interpret* the often vague information provided by patients will be essential if an EMT-B intends to use a complaint-based approach effectively (**Figure 3-1**).

The Progression of Cardiac Disease

angina
Transient (short-lived) chest discomfort caused by partial or temporary blockage of blood flow to the heart muscle.

unstable angina
Angina that involves increasing pain, occurs more frequently, and responds less and less to nitroglycerin.

For the patient with classic <u>angina</u> (exercise-induced ischemia), a chief complaint of *pain or discomfort* is common. However, some patients will complain of weakness or confusion as a result of their progressing cardiac disease. In fact, between 4 and 5 million patients a year, many brought to the hospital by ambulance, will be treated because of these very complaints of weakness or confusion. About 40% of these patients will be diagnosed as having acute ischemic disease. Another 10% will be diagnosed with <u>unstable angina</u>, while still another 30% will have an acute myocardial infarction (AMI). Of the patients who are actually having a myocardial infarction, one third of them will die within the first hour of symptom onset. Therefore, chest pain or discomfort should *always* be taken as a serious complaint. The statistics bear out the need for care providers to be tuned in to this, because the mortality rate for patients presenting with their first prolonged episode of ischemic chest pain is about 34%. For roughly half of those patients, *this initial pain presentation is their only symptom prior to dying!*

The onset of the pain or discomfort of angina usually is associated with exertion or stress of some kind and may be described as a dull, squeezing feeling, tightness, or pressure in the chest. The pain may or may not radiate to the jaw or left arm. The severity of pain does not necessarily correlate to the severity of the patient's ischemia. Patients who are experiencing classic angina are commonly diaphoretic and may have additional complaints of difficulty breathing or shortness of breath, and possibly be nauseated or vomit. Patients may allude to having heart palpitations, sometimes saying that they feel like there are "butterflies in their chest." In the absence of a medical background, keep in mind that patients will draw from their vocabulary and life experience to describe what they perceive is happening. You may hear comments such as "I just feel different" or "I have this funny feeling." Again, you must be able to interpret their words into medical terms. Avoid the danger of discounting the potential severity of a patient's condition simply because the patient doesn't use accurate medical terminology.

As coronary disease progresses, the angina a patient experiences will at some point transition from being classified as stable to unstable. When this occurs, there is typically a change in the pattern. Patients may experience an increase in the *frequency* or length of their episodes or attacks as well as in the degree of pain/discomfort being experienced. Although exertion may still precipitate the problem, patients may not recognize the seemingly small activity preceding the attack as exertion. You may hear a patient say "I went to the porch to get the paper, and I couldn't catch my breath."

Complaints of fainting, weakness, dizziness, or confusion should be considered as possible warning signs any time cardiac disease is involved. With the evolution of cardiac disease also comes an increase in the *severity* of the attacks or episodes. Failure of rest or prescribed medications to relieve the patient's symptoms indicates a heart in need of oxygen and a delivery system that is incapable of meeting that basic

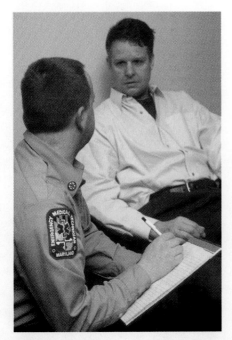

Figure 3-1 The patient's initial response to the question "What's wrong?" is the chief complaint.

metabolic need. With increasing cardiac ischemia, AMI and possibly sudden cardiac death may be imminent.

> ## Training Tip
>
> Try to arrange a clinical rotation through your local EMS training institution to observe a percutaneous transluminal coronary angioplasty (PTCA) in the catheterization lab at a local hospital.

Assessment of the Cardiac Patient

Without question, identifying the chief complaint and obtaining an accurate history are key contributions from the field setting. Of the common chief complaints (Table 3-1), chest pain or discomfort is most commonly associated with AMI. One of the keys to obtaining an accurate history in as short a time as possible is to use a standardized approach. This ensures that all the right questions are asked. A classic model is the OPQRST approach when assessing a patient complaining of chest pain (Table 3-2).

Table 3-1: Common Chief Complaints

- Chest pain/pressure
- Indigestion
- Discomfort
- Difficulty breathing
- Weakness
- Fainting
- Palpitations

Table 3-2: The OPQRST of Pain

O—Onset

Key Question: What were you doing when the pain/discomfort started?

P—Provoke/Palliation

Key Question: What makes the pain/discomfort better or worse? What have you tried to reduce the symptoms? Nitroglycerin? Antacids? Rest? Did they work?

Support Questions: Has this ever happened before? If so, when?

Q—Quality

Key Question: What does the pain feel like (squeezing, burning, heaviness)?

R—Region/Radiation

Key Question: Can you point with one finger to the main area of pain/discomfort?

Support Questions: Do you feel pain anywhere else? If so, can you show me or tell me where it is?

S—Severity

Key Question: How bad is the pain on a scale of 1 to 10, with 1 being no pain and 10 being extreme pain?

Support Questions: What is the worst pain you've ever experienced? How does this compare?

T—Timeframes

Key Question: When did you first notice the symptoms?

Support Questions: Have the symptoms been continuous? If not, has the feeling come and gone?

Table 3-3: The Six Steps of Reading the Patient
Observe—Assess level of consciousness, patient location/position, skin color, activity level, and general level of distress.
Talk—Identify the chief complaint or the reason for the call. (Is the problem new or a recurrence of an old one?) Determine airway patency and level of consciousness.
Touch—Assess skin temperature/moisture and pulse parameters.
Auscultate—Listen to breath sounds, and assess overall adequacy of breathing.
Identify—Find and correct any immediate life threats.
Assess—Obtain a complete and accurate set of vital signs.

Given the basic template of OPQRST, you can use the same basic questions to elicit a history based on a complaint of difficulty breathing, weakness, discomfort, or even feeling funny. In fact, with simple modifications, you can use this tool with virtually any chief complaint. This will allow you to identify and prioritize the most pressing problems, which in turn facilitates a better care plan.

Another good model to incorporate into your basic assessment is the six-step approach to "reading the patient" (Table 3-3).

You should start to read a patient from the moment you walk in the room. The process continues as you make initial contact and introduce yourself and your partner. When you shake the patient's hand and feel for a pulse, you also can assess the patient's skin condition. The look in your patient's eyes and that person's verbal response to your entry also contribute to your initial impression. Within 20 seconds, you should have an idea as to whether the patient is sick or not. Nonetheless, the condition of a cardiac patient can change from being stable one minute to unstable the next, so it is important to reassess the patient continually throughout the call.

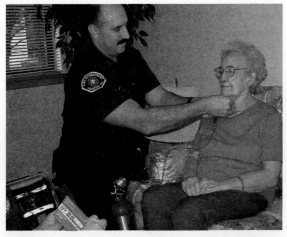

Figure 3-2 Oxygen therapy should be initiated by the EMT-B at the first indication that the patient's condition might be cardiac in origin or that the patient is being deprived of oxygen for any reason.

Key Concepts of Emergency Cardiac Care

There are four fundamental goals in emergency cardiac care. These goals reach across the borders of field medicine into the hospital setting. EMT-Bs, EMT-Is, EMT-Ps, nurses, and physicians must work collectively to meet these goals and contribute to the success of the overall patient care effort.

1. **Prevent or Correct Hypoxia**—Oxygen therapy should be initiated by the EMT-B at the first indication that the patient's condition might be cardiac in origin or that the patient is being deprived of oxygen for any reason (**Figure 3-2**). Although a nasal cannula may be less restrictive and seemingly better tolerated by the patient, the concentrations of delivered oxygen using that particular device are relatively low—a maximum of

about 36%. Whether the patient presents with the anxious, skittish behavior often found with early hypoxia or the markedly decreased level of consciousness associated with more serious levels of hypoxia, corrective intervention needs to occur as soon as possible. To that end, 12 to 15 L/min of oxygen delivered via nonrebreathing mask will deliver close to 100% oxygen and turn most hypoxia around quickly. For the patient who seems hesitant to use the mask, direct yet empathetic communications to encourage its use often will result in patient compliance. The mask allows you to deliver almost *three times* the concentration of oxygen as a nasal cannula.

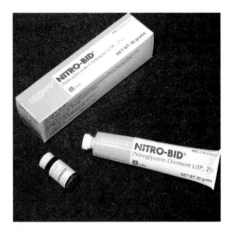

Figure 3-3 The use of various nitrate preparations has been repeatedly shown to be beneficial in emergency cardiac care.

2. **Improve Myocardial Blood Flow**—The use of various nitrate preparations has been repeatedly shown to be beneficial in emergency cardiac care (**Figure 3-3**). Improved blood flow to the heart, specifically to the areas immediately surrounding the infarct or ischemic tissue, is the primary goal. With its vasodilating effects, nitroglycerin helps to decrease the workload of the left ventricle, which directly reduces the heart's oxygen consumption. At the same time, it increases coronary blood flow, which also is very desirable. With more and more EMT-Bs having the capability to administer nitroglycerin, administration of this key cardiac drug should not be delayed. Irrespective of who administers nitrates, the patient's blood pressure needs to be carefully monitored to prevent it from becoming too low.

   The EMT-B should obtain frequent blood pressure measurements when patients are receiving nitrates and more frequently if the drugs are being administered by IV infusion, which increases the risk of "bottoming out" the patient's blood pressure.

3. **Reduce Pain and Anxiety**—Various analgesics are used to reduce pain and anxiety in cardiac patients. Morphine or self-administered nitrous oxide, used alone or in conjunction with morphine, provides excellent analgesia. Morphine is the most common drug of choice because it is effective against the extreme pain and anxiety associated with AMI. In some cases, it is not uncommon for a cardiac patient to receive 20 mg or more of morphine between the field and initial evaluation in the emergency department. Although morphine dosing in this range may only relieve the pain partially and make a cardiac patient somewhat less anxious, the same dose might well render a patient with another condition unconscious.

   With increased or ongoing dosing of morphine comes an increased risk of central nervous system and respiratory depression. The EMT-B must be alert for any changes in the patient's level of consciousness and must continually evaluate the adequacy of breathing (**Figure 3-4**). Be prepared to quickly step in and assist with ventilations should the need arise.

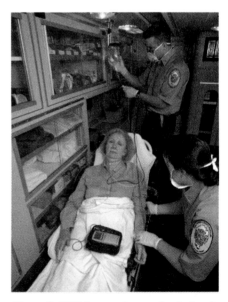

Figure 3-4 With increased or ongoing dosing of morphine, the EMT-B needs to be alert for any changes in the patient's level of consciousness and must continually evaluate the adequacy of breathing.

4. **Control Heart Rate and Blood Pressure**—Expect ALS or hospital staff to use drugs called beta-blockers for many patients with suspected AMI. This family of drugs has the ability to decrease heart rate, drop the systolic blood pressure, and block the effects of the sympathetic nervous system, which makes them good choices in

cardiac care. Again, the EMT-B can positively contribute to patient care by being aware of a patient's vital signs and level of consciousness whenever these drugs are being administered (**Figure 3-5**). If changes in the patient's condition are noted, make certain that the team leader knows what is going on by being specific. For example, indicate that the patient is no longer responding when spoken to.

As with most emergency medicine, excellent patient assessment skills and a focus on performing the basic fundamental components of patient care as flawlessly as possible will help to ensure the best outcome for the patient. Early access to ALS whenever possible and/or rapid, safe transport to the appropriate facility also are essential considerations. Finally, never forget that it often is the team's cohesiveness that may determine the success of its efforts.

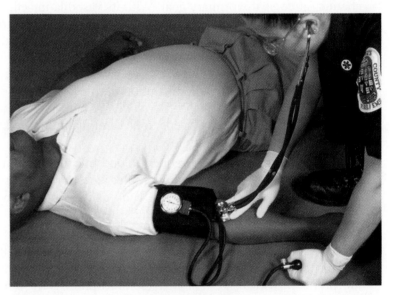

Figure 3-5 The EMT-B can positively contribute to patient care by keeping a close eye on the patient's vital signs and level of consciousness.

Wrap Up

Chapter 3
From Angina to AMI:
The Cardiac Care Continuum

Ready for Review

In this chapter, you have learned the range of cardiac conditions that may be encountered in the field. You also have seen how critical your job is to the patient's overall cardiac care—from the 9-1-1 call to the cardiac catheterization lab. Especially important in this chapter are the key questions you will be using to help find out the patient's state (complaint-based analysis). As an informed EMT-B, you can now see that your observation and analysis begin the moment you arrive on the scene and continue through to the hand-off to hospital staff.

Quick Case

1) Your squad is dispatched to a retirement home where you find a 75-year-old woman complaining of chest discomfort. Her caregiver tells you that the patient has been treated for angina for the last 3 years with limited problems. However, over the last several months, the frequency of her angina attacks has increased and appear to be getting more severe. In addition, she felt no relief from three sprays of her sublingual nitroglycerin.

This information makes you suspect that this patient is at high risk for what event?

_____

_____

2) A man in the checkout line at the grocery store collapses, prompting a call to 9-1-1. By the time EMS is on scene, the patient is conscious and seated on the floor, still in obvious distress. You apply a high concentration of oxygen, which improves the patient's color immediately. As you wait for ALS to arrive, what essential information should you attempt to obtain from the patient?

_____

_____

_____

Rhythms of the Heart

*T**his chapter is designed to teach you the key rhythms of the heart and how to recognize each rhythm on ECG strips or your team's heart monitor screen. You will learn the separate parts of the heart's electrical activity on the ECG paper and what they represent. You will learn what some of the key abnormal rhythms are, what they do to your patient, and how to attempt to correct them. You will also learn how to recognize mechanical and electrical interference with your heart monitor and how to eliminate these equipment problems.*

Due to the limited scope of ACLS for EMT-Bs, this chapter focuses on the skill of analyzing and interpreting basic ECG rhythm strips. From the perspective of an EMT-B working in the field, the most important concepts relative to cardiac rhythms are the following:

- Understanding the impact of fast and slow heart rates
- Grasping the difference between electrical and mechanical activity in the heart
- Being able to differentiate between regular, irregular, and *regularly* irregular rhythms
- Recognizing the three lethal cardiac rhythms: ventricular fibrillation, ventricular tachycardia, and asystole
- Understanding the concept of cardiac rhythms falling under the heading of pulseless electrical activity (PEA)
- Being able to identify artifact and, when possible, correct the problem

The Pump of a Lifetime

The anatomic design and capabilities of the human heart are remarkable (**Figure 4-1**). This four-chamber muscular pump with a series of valves to control blood flow is driven by a specialized electrical conduction system (**Figure 4-2**). There are even backup pacemaker sites should the primary pacemaker of the heart fail. These are all desirable features, since we count on our heart to beat for a lifetime.

In order to accomplish its task, the heart has a specialized cellular structure and features. To better understand its function, you must first understand the four unique properties of the heart (Table 4-1).

There are working cells within the heart that normally maintain an electrical charge across their cell walls; they are said to be polarized. Think of this polarized state as a state of readiness. When an electric current stimulates these working cells, they electrically discharge and are said to have depolarized. The process of depolarization makes the muscle filaments contract and shortens the cell length, which is what makes the heart pump.

Within the heart are also found a second type of cell called electrical cells. These cells have a dual role, acting as the primary and backup pacemakers of the heart and also forming part of the wiring or conduction system that moves the electrical impulses throughout the heart.

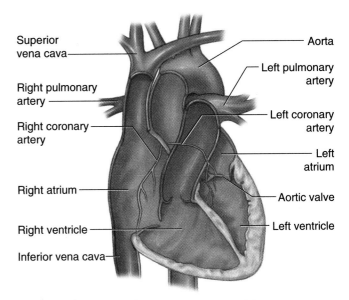

Figure 4-1 The human heart.

Table 4-1: The Properties of Cardiac Muscle

- **Automaticity** – The heart has the ability to initiate electrical impulses spontaneously without outside stimulation.

- **Excitability** – The cells that make up the heart are able to respond to these electrical impulses.

- **Conductivity** – These impulses travel through a type of internal wiring system throughout the heart.

- **Contractility** – The cardiac muscle responds to electrical stimulation by contracting and pumping blood throughout the body.

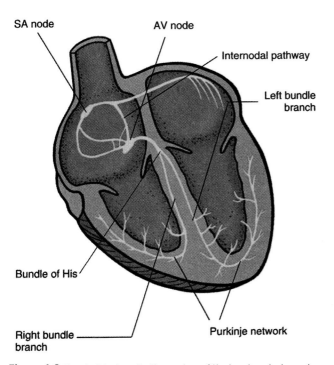

Figure 4-2 The electrical conduction system of the heart controls most aspects of heart rate and enables the four chambers to work together.

The heart has other physical capabilities that allow it to better perform its essential life functions. For example, the heart, in conjunction with the autonomic nervous system, can either speed up or slow down the heart rate as well as adjust the strength of its contractions based on the body's momentary metabolic needs. This gives the heart tremendous latitude in its performance potential.

Involuntary actions of the body, such as breathing, digestion, and heart function, are controlled by the autonomic nervous system, which is broken down into two parts: the sympathetic and parasympathetic nervous systems.

The sympathetic nervous system is primarily concerned with ensuring that the body is prepared to handle assorted stressors encountered on a daily basis. Also known as the "fight or flight" system, the sympathetic nervous system speeds up the heart rate and controls the strength of contractions.

Of course, there must be a counterpart to this process so that the heart doesn't beat too fast all the time and wear out too early. The parasympathetic nervous system is that counterpart. Its main job is to monitor the body's vegetative functions and slow the body and the heart down once the stressor that stimulated the sympathetic nervous system is gone.

A comparison of the two systems is shown in Table 4-2.

With this basic understanding of cardiac physiology, let's continue and learn the fundamentals of analyzing some of the key cardiac rhythms and the process of monitoring them.

Table 4-2: Comparison of Sympathetic and Parasympathetic Nervous Systems

Sympathetic	Parasympathetic
Speeds up the heart	Slows down the heart
Dilates the pupils	Constricts the pupils
Constricts blood vessels	Dilates blood vessels (increases salivation)
Raises blood pressure	Lowers blood pressure, controls gastrointestinal activity

The Fundamentals of Cardiac Rhythm Analysis

electrocardiogram (ECG)
A tracing on graph paper that represents the electrical activity of the heart.

An **electrocardiogram (ECG)** is a tracing made on graph paper that is moved past a heated stylus at a fixed speed (**Figure 4-3**). What is recorded on the paper represents the electrical activity of the heart. An ECG does not evaluate whether the patient has any corresponding mechanical activity, ie, heart contractions, a palpable pulse, or a blood pressure.

As electrical events occur in the heart and are recorded, they occupy a certain amount of space on the graph paper. This space represents a measurement of time. The time it takes for each event to occur is compared to baseline values for each event, which in turn represents the identifying features of the various cardiac rhythms.

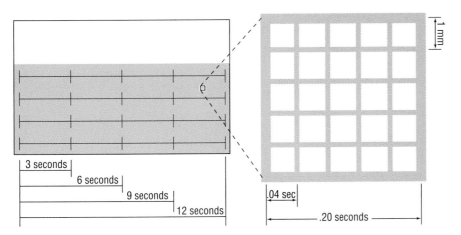

Figure 4-3 ECG paper.

Each small box on the ECG graph paper represents 0.04 seconds. Five of these small boxes make up a large box, representing 0.20 seconds. Collectively, five of the large boxes represent 1.0 second. Although the actual mark may differ, all ECG papers contain identifying marks every 3 seconds to serve as a reference.

The primary pacemaker of the heart is the **sinoatrial (SA) node**, often called the sinus node. It is a collection of specialized electrical cells located high in the upper right corner of the right atrium.Approximately once every second, the SA node initiates an electrical impulse. This impulse normally moves down the intra-atrial conduction pathways and depolarizes the atria (producing the P wave on the ECG). The impulse is slowed briefly as it passes the junction between the atria and the ventricles (the atrioventricular [AV] junction) and continues down to the ventricles. Once the impulse passes the AV junction, it moves through the Bundle of His, and then splits into the left and right bundle branches. Finally, the impulse makes its way through the Purkinje system, at which point it is delivered to the musculature of the ventricles, causing them to depolarize and contract, producing the QRS complex on the ECG.

The heart then readies itself to repeat the process. This recovery or readiness period is represented on the ECG by the T wave. Each PQRST wave segment equates with one complete cardiac cycle, and as these electrical events occur, they are traced onto the ECG paper (**Figure 4-4**). The varying size of each component is dependent on the amount of electrical amplitude. Under normal circumstances, each cardiac cycle results in contraction of the heart and the production of a corresponding pulse, brought about by the small electrical impulse generated by the SA node (**Figure 4-5**). The journey that each impulse must take is even more amazing when you consider that, in times of stress or exertion, the *entire process* may be occurring *two or three times every second!*

To be able to analyze an ECG quickly and correctly requires a consistent, systematic approach. You should

sinoatrial node
A collection of specialized electrical cells located high in the upper right corner of the right atrium that is the primary pacemaker of the heart; also called the sinus node.

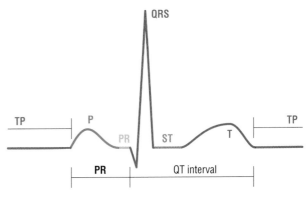

Figure 4-4 Each PQRST wave segment equates with one complete cardiac cycle, and as these electrical events occur, they are traced onto the ECG paper.

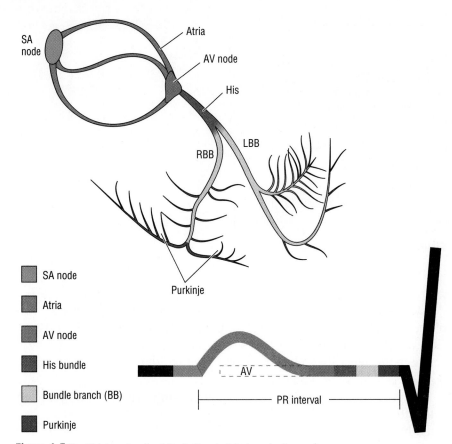

Figure 4-5 The PR interval as it relates to the electrical conduction system.

evaluate each ECG *exactly* the same way, looking at *exactly* the same components *every* time. While you will only be learning a few of the literally dozens of cardiac rhythms, it is still essential that you use a standardized approach. Consistency is the key to a successful interpretation.

You will be learning the same rhythm analysis format as more advanced providers but will be focusing your efforts differently. For example, while you will still learn to recognize a "PR interval," you will not be required to measure it. This basic understanding will provide a foundation on which to improve your capabilities as an EMT-B working in an advanced cardiac life support setting.

We will be breaking down the ECG rhythm interpretation format into two steps. Step 1 involves two distinct components: evaluating the heart rate and the rhythm.

- Is the patient's rate less than 60 or greater than 100?
- Is the pulse that you are feeling regular, irregular, or regularly irregular?

Step 2 of your rhythm analysis looks at these additional components:

- Are P waves present, upright, and in a 1:1 ratio to each QRS complex?
- Does the PR interval appear to be within normal limits?
- Does the duration of the QRS complex appear to be within normal limits?
- Does this appear to be a lethal rhythm?

Step 1 of Rhythm Analysis

Assessing Heart Rate

The tallest point in a normal ECG is the top of the QRS complex (the R wave). Given that this represents the electrical depolarization of the ventricles, the largest and most muscular aspect of the heart, it only makes sense that this would be the largest electrical representation on the ECG.

The quickest and simplest way to measure heart rate is to count the number of R waves in a 6-second strip and then multiply that number by 10. This would give you a good estimate of the heart rate for a minute. Of course, you have to check a pulse to make certain that the electrical activity you are seeing on the cardiac monitor is actually producing a pulse. Evaluation of the rate and regularity of a patient's pulse can and should be accomplished by an EMT-B without the use of a cardiac monitor.

Calculate the heart rate in the ECG rhythm strips in **Figure 4-6.**

For most adults, the normal heart rate usually is between 60 and 100 beats/min. Remember that these are only baseline numbers based on the intrinsic firing rate of the primary pacemaker of the heart, the SA node. A distance runner who is in excellent physical condition may have a normal resting pulse of 48 beats/min, well below the low-end rate of 60 beats/min. By comparison, an overweight, heavy smoker may have a resting pulse rate of 110 beats/min. This textbook will focus on average people using baseline numbers for comparison.

Any time the heart rate rises, there usually is a proportionate increase in blood pressure. Of course, when the work of the heart is increased to meet the metabolic needs of the body, the needs of the heart increase as well. In the case of a patient with a diseased heart, this is a potentially lethal combination. The heart, despite its physical state, whether it is diseased or damaged from a myocardial infarction, will still attempt to respond to the needs of the body. If the disease or damage is so extensive

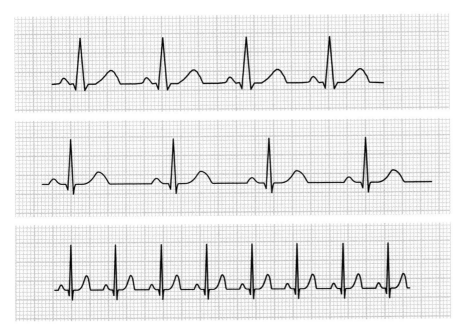

Figure 4-6 Calculate the heart rate in these ECG rhythm strips.

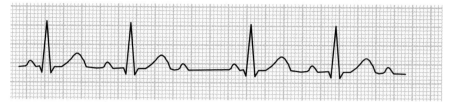

Figure 4-7 An example of a regularly irregular rhythm.

that the heart cannot perform its metabolic functions, heart failure is likely to occur.

In situations in which the heart beats extremely fast or slow, another phenomenon occurs. At some point when the heart rate exceeds about 170 or 180 beats/min, there is not enough time for the chambers of the heart to fill between each contraction. Because of this, cardiac output decreases, in turn causing a drop in blood pressure. By comparison, slow heart rates in the low 40s or high 30s also result in decreased cardiac output and a corresponding fall in blood pressure.

Assessing Regularity

The rhythms of the heart fall into one of three categories: regular, irregular, or regularly irregular. Most of the rhythms produced by the heart are regular. As such, any time an irregular pulse is noted, there is cause for concern. Granted, some irregular heart rhythms are not lethal, but as a general rule, *not regular* equates with *not normal,* and it is prudent patient care to assume that the situation is *not good.*

If you encounter a patient who has a rhythm that is not regular but has a pattern, that rhythm is termed as regularly irregular (**Figure 4-7**). Consider a few possibilities when this happens. First, an ectopic pacemaker of the heart may be creating impulses in addition to those created by the SA node. These two competing pacemakers can confuse the heart, as it will potentially respond to *any impulse,* irrespective of origin, assuming that the heart is polarized and in a state of readiness.

Second, a certain portion of the impulses may not be making their way through the conduction system. When this happens, the impulses are said to have been "blocked." Any blocked impulse that does not reach and depolarize the ventricles results in a missed beat. If this blocking occurs with a pattern, the missed or dropped beats can result in the pattern associated with "regular irregularity."

Whatever the cause of regularly irregular cardiac rhythms, this situation is not normal and could point to a worsening cardiac condition. When this is observed, either call for an ALS response or rendezvous. If neither of those options is available, provide immediate emergency transport to the hospital (**Figure 4-8**).

Step 2 of Rhythm Analysis

To become proficient at identifying and evaluating the components of the ECG that will be described next requires additional training and practice outside this course. However, the fundamentals and key con-

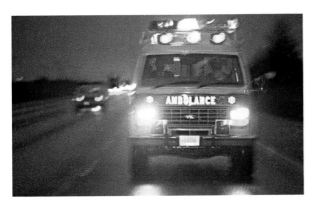

Figure 4-8 Provide immediate emergency transport to the hospital for patients with regularly irregular cardiac rhythms.

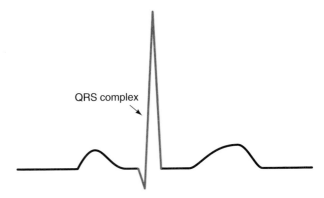

Figure 4-9 Each P wave should be followed by one QRS complex.

cepts that are presented will serve as an excellent foundation on which to build if you choose to continue your studies.

In recollection, the SA node is located in the upper right portion of the heart. Given the angle and anatomic position of the heart (turned with the base or ventricle slightly tipped forward), the normal conduction path of each impulse flows from the upper right down to the lower left. If you draw an imaginary line from your right shoulder down to your left hip, you are close to tracking the axis of the heart's conduction system. The most common lead configuration used in the prehospital setting is lead II, which parallels the conduction system. In this lead, the components of the ECG, the P wave, the QRS complex, and the T wave are upright on the rhythm strip.

An upright P wave in lead II implies that the primary pacemaker of the heart, the SA node, is in control. Again, a rate between 60 and 100 beats/min is normal, with a top-end performance of about 150 beats/min.

Each P wave should be followed by one QRS complex (**Figure 4-9**). If more P waves exist than QRS complexes, some of the impulses are possibly being *blocked* and not depolarizing the ventricles. If no P waves are present, this usually indicates that some other pacemaker is functioning as the driving force of the heart.

The normal time lapse for each impulse generated by the SA node to move through the atria and depolarize them is 0.12 to 0.20 seconds (three to five small boxes). If it takes longer than that for each impulse to reach the AV junction, there is some type of conduction problem (**Figure 4-10**). If you note this, it is best to err on the patient's side. Assume that something is amiss and watch the patient carefully.

Next, evaluate the QRS complex, which represents the time it takes for the electrical impulse to move through the AV junction and through the ventricles. The QRS complex should be no more than 0.10 seconds ($2\frac{1}{2}$ small boxes). If the QRS complex is wider than 0.10 seconds, an intraventricular conduction delay (IVCD) is present. This can be the result of a variety of causes, including heart muscle damaged by a heart attack, a chemical imbalance, or assorted drugs. At the EMT-B level, the cause of the IVCD is not the issue. Noting the wide QRS complex is

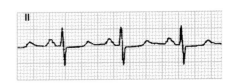

Figure 4-10 If it takes longer than 0.20 seconds for each impulse to reach the AV junction, there is a conduction problem.

what is important. More importantly, always keep in mind that you are there to treat the patient, not the cardiac monitor. Learning more about rhythm strips will broaden your knowledge as an EMT-B but is a hindrance if it distracts you from providing good patient care.

Training Tip

Have your ALS provider save copies of ECGs for you. Occasionally, at a training session, pass them around and let the crew members on your squad look them over.

---

normal sinus rhythm (NSR)
A rhythm that occurs when the electrical activity of the heart and the intervals on the ECG are within normal limits.

sinus bradycardia
A common rhythm that is normal except that the rate is slower than normal.

sinus tachycardia
A common rhythm that is normal except that the rate is faster than normal.

ventricular fibrillation (VF)
A rhythm that occurs when the ventricles quiver rather than contract; the most common rhythm in sudden cardiac arrest.

ventricular tachycardia (VT)
A rhythm in which the ventricular rate is very fast; the heart is working very hard; may or may not produce a pulse.

asystole
A total absence of electrical and mechanical activity in the heart; also called flatline.

Table 4-3: Sinus Bradycardia

Common causes:

- Increased parasympathetic tone
- Drug toxicity
- Damage to the heart's conduction system

What to watch for:

- Altered level of responsiveness/confusion
- Decreased blood pressure level
- Ectopic beats (any abnormal beats)

Cardiac Rhythms
What Is Normal Sinus Rhythm?

When impulses from the SA node pace the heart and the cardiac rhythm's components are within normal limits, the rhythm is called **normal sinus rhythm (NSR)**. This is the foundation cardiac rhythm and is unique to itself. The identifying features of NSR include the following:

- Regular rhythm
- Heart rate of 60 to 100 beats/min
- P waves that are upright, in a 1:1 ratio, preceding each QRS complex
- PR interval of $\leq$ 0.12 to 0.20 seconds
- QRS complex of $\leq$ 0.10 seconds

The other two sinus rhythms that commonly occur are **sinus bradycardia** and **sinus tachycardia**. The *only* thing that differentiates these two variations of sinus rhythm from the parent rhythm of NSR is the rate. Aside from that, the identifying features of each of the three rhythms are the same. In the case of sinus bradycardia, the heart rate is less than 60 beats/min. By comparison, sinus tachycardia has a rate of greater than 100 beats/min. Because of the frequency with which all three of these rhythms present, it is helpful if you know something about what can cause them as well as be able to recognize them.

Sinus bradycardia can in fact be a normal rhythm in young persons with healthy hearts (Table 4-3).

Sinus tachycardia is considered a classic warning arrhythmia (Table 4-4). The rhythm in itself is not treated. The goal with this rhythm is to find its underlying cause and treat it when possible.

The Lethal Three

Ventricular fibrillation (VF), **ventricular tachycardia (VT)**, and **asystole** are cardiac rhythms considered to be lethal for good reason. Two of the three, ventricular fibrillation and asystole, do not produce pulses, which means the patient is in cardiac arrest. The third, ventricular tachycardia, is a bit more complex in that it may or may not produce a pulse. In the cases where ventricular tachycardia is producing a pulse, it usually is not a rhythm that the heart can sustain for extended periods. At some point, maybe in 1 minute or in 30 minutes, ventricular tachycardia usually deteriorates into ventricular fibrillation and the patient has a cardiac arrest. In other cases, ventricular tachycardia is the presenting rhythm but is pulseless. When this occurs, the condition is treated *exactly* like ventricular fibrillation.

Ventricular Fibrillation

This is the most common presenting rhythm in sudden cardiac arrest, and when it occurs, the ventricles quiver rather than contract, resulting in no cardiac output and no pulse. When ventricular fibrillation is noted, the patient should be assessed immediately to rule out muscle tremors, patient movement, loose lead artifact, or seizure activity.

If the rhythm is ventricular fibrillation and the onset is recent, it will usually appear choppy (**Figure 4-11**). As time passes, the frequency and amplitude progressively decrease, producing what is termed *fine ventricular fibrillation*. If left untreated, ventricular fibrillation will eventually degrade into asystole. The identifying features of ventricular fibrillation are as follows:

- Heart rate cannot be determined
- Rhythm is grossly irregular
- No P waves
- No PR interval
- No QRS complex (replaced by choppy fibrillation waves)

Treatment. Once the patient is confirmed as pulseless and apneic, initial treatment depends on whether or not a defibrillator is available. If a defibrillator is available, it should be applied immediately and the patient defibrillated. When a defibrillator is not available, CPR should be initiated and high concentrations of oxygen provided during ventilations.

Ventricular Tachycardia

Ventricular tachycardia (**Figure 4-12**) is a dangerous, unstable rhythm. Although it can produce a pulse, in many cases it does not. When ventricular tachycardia does produce a pulse, it usually is not strong. A heart in this

Table 4-4: Sinus Tachycardia
Common causes:
• Pain
• Fear/anxiety
• Fever
• Drug use (prescription, over-the-counter, or illicit)
• Shock/trauma/hypovolemia
• Dehydration
What to watch for:
• Chest pain/palpitations
• Headache
• Blood pressure changes

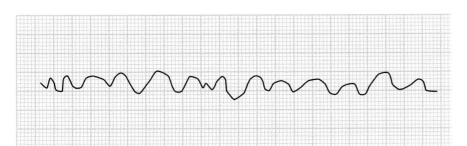

Figure 4-11 Ventricular fibrillation appears choppy at the onset.

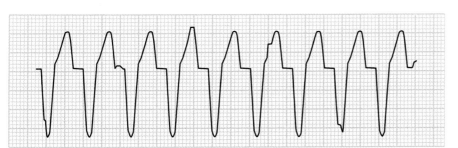

Figure 4-12 Ventricular tachycardia.

rhythm is working hard and has very high oxygen needs. Given the fact that there probably is preexisting heart disease often complicated by the current cardiac crisis, it is of little surprise that this rhythm usually is a transition rhythm, frequently deteriorating into ventricular fibrillation within a few minutes. The identifying features of ventricular tachycardia are as follows:

- Heart rate of 100 to 250 beats/min
- Usually regular rhythm
- Usually no P waves
- No PR interval
- QRS complex is wide, bizarre (greater than 0.12 seconds); often looks like large Vs side by side

Treatment. If the patient is alert with no signs of decreased cardiac output, you may see the ALS team administer high-flow oxygen, if not done already by the BLS team, and then start an IV, while attempting to correct the problem by suppressing the rhythm with medication. If the patient is symptomatic with chest pain, decreased level of consciousness, hypotension, or cool clammy skin, expect to see a synchronized countershock (cardioversion). If time permits, the patient will be sedated for two reasons. First, this frightening situation becomes uncomfortable at best and painful at worst as the frequency or the voltage of the countershocks increases. Second, sedation improves the likelihood that the procedure will be successful.

On occasion, patients will go into a form of ventricular tachycardia that does not produce any pulses, ie, pulseless ventricular tachycardia. Again, when this occurs, the rhythm is treated exactly like ventricular fibrillation.

Asystole

Whether it is called asystole, flatline, or cardiac standstill, this type of cardiac malfunction represents an absence of electrical and mechanical activity in the heart (**Figure 4-13**). When an adult patient presents in asystole, the prognosis is ominous.

The identifying features of asystole are as follows:

- No heart rate
- No rhythm
- No P waves
- No PR interval
- No QRS complex

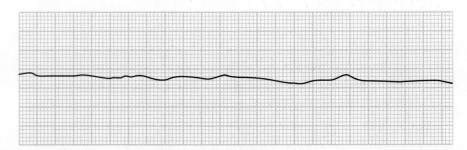

Figure 4-13 Asystole.

Treatment. The first phase of treating asystole is to confirm that the patient's heart is in that state. The patient should be pulseless and apneic. In addition, a four-part check should be performed that includes the following:

- **Contact** — Make certain that the monitoring electrodes are securely attached to the skin by firmly pressing on them.
- **Connection** — Check that the patient cable is plugged securely into the cardiac monitor.
- **Calibration** — Make sure that the automatic gain control (AGC) wasn't accidentally turned off or down.
- **Check another lead** — Manually change the lead selection on the cardiac monitor to assess the rhythm in another lead and to be sure the monitor is set to the right selection, ie, leads vs. quick look paddles.

It is essential that the rhythm be confirmed because treatments for each of the various cardiac rhythms can differ drastically.

With ventricular fibrillation, some electrical activity is present in the heart. It needs to be controlled and then converted into a perfusing rhythm. With asystole, because there is no electrical or mechanical activity, CPR must be instituted quickly followed by drug therapy in hopes of stimulating the heart to respond. Occasionally, you will see the heart paced externally, but this rarely works. If you think of how serious the condition of a given patient has to be in order to reduce the heart to a total shutdown, it makes sense that there is, at best, a slim hope of resuscitation.

Training Tip

Have an in-service where your ALS provider takes you through the various functions of the four-part asystole check.

If the EMT-B can do this type of check on a call, patient care is improved by freeing up the paramedic to perform other ALS functions such as intubation, gaining IV access, or administering drugs.

Pulseless Electrical Activity

Sometimes a patient will present in a cardiac rhythm that produces an ECG tracing but does not produce a corresponding pulse. In theory, almost any cardiac rhythm could be **pulseless electrical activity (PEA)**, which is why it is so important to ensure that your patient has a pulse even when the ECG tracing shows electrical activity. However, in many cases, the rhythm that is resulting in PEA is slow and has a wide QRS complex. As one might guess, PEA is a sign that may reflect serious damage to the heart. There are some treatable causes of PEA, but they are outside the scope of this text.

pulseless electrical activity (PEA)
A rhythm that occurs when there is electrical activity in the heart but no pulse.

Artifact

For a clean, easily readable ECG to be produced, various technical aspects of cardiac monitoring must be in place and working properly. If any of the following occur, the quality of the tracing may range from marginal to unreadable due to **artifact**, which in turn may contribute to

artifact
A wave on the ECG that results from something other than the electrical activity of the heart.

Table 4-5: Causes and Corrective Measures for Artifact	
Cause/Condition	Corrective Actions
Poor electrode contact (wet or loose)	Dry any wet skin. If the electrode is loose, push it down firmly. Consider replacing the electrode.
Poor electrode contact (hairy skin)	Shave the chest area where the electrodes should be placed.
Loose lead	Snap the lead wire onto the back of the electrode.
Dry electrode	Replace the electrode with a new one.
Patient movement	Encourage the patient to be still.
Muscle tremor	If the patient is shivering, try to warm him or her. Confirm that seizure activity is not present.
60-cycle interference	Find the cause and unplug or shut it off. Common causes include heating pads, electric blankets, and microwave ovens.

less than optimal patient care (Table 4-5). Also, remember that leads need to be placed correctly in order to obtain a correct ECG reading (Figure 4-14).

Cardiac monitoring is a straightforward diagnostic procedure that provides important information about the overall function and stability of a patient's heart at a given moment. The ability to get the patient hooked up quickly is another valuable function that the EMT-B can perform. In any case, cardiac monitoring is a key element of emergency cardiac care, because lethal arrhythmias are a common cause of death in these patients.

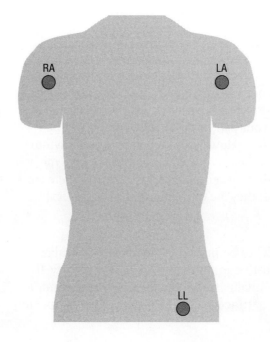

Figure 4-14 Standard lead II placement.

Wrap Up

**Chapter 4
Rhythms of the Heart**

Ready for Review

This chapter introduced you to the rhythms of the heart and showed you how to recognize each rhythm on an ECG strip or on the heart monitor screen. You know now the definitions of ventricular fibrillation, ventricular tachycardia, and asystole and why they are called "the lethal three." You know how to attach electrodes to your patient's skin, some common error readings, and how to check faulty leads and equipment. The next chapter offers a more in-depth review of the electrical interventions used in emergency cardiac care.

Quick Case

1. You arrive at the scene of a 56-year-old woman complaining of crushing chest pain. Upon noting that she has a very slow heart rate and hypotension, you place her on 100% oxygen and request an ALS ambulance. When the paramedics arrive, they place the patient on the cardiac monitor, which displays a sinus bradycardia at a rate of 44 beats/min.

   What is the correlation between this patient's bradycardia and her low blood pressure?

   _____

   _____

2. After assessing an elderly man as being unstable, you and your partner decide to arrange a rendezvous with an ALS ambulance because the closest hospital is approximately 30 miles away. When you meet the paramedics and begin assisting them with their care, you are asked to place the patient on a cardiac monitor. The ECG appears to indicate ventricular fibrillation, yet the patient is awake and talking.

   Why is this *not* possible?

   What would you do to troubleshoot the problem?

   _____

   _____

3. You are the EMT-B assisting a paramedic in the back of an ALS ambulance while transporting an unconscious patient to the hospital. IV therapy has already been initiated and the patient is on 100% oxygen. The cardiac monitor is displaying a normal sinus rhythm at a rate of 80 beats/min. The paramedic asks you to palpate for a carotid pulse. What is the rationale for this request if the patient has a normal cardiac rhythm?

   _____

   _____

   _____

5

Electrical Interventions in Cardiac Care

This chapter introduces the student to the indications for the use of electrical interventions and explains the function of a defibrillator and how it is properly used. Three types of defibrillators are described as well as cardiac pacemakers. The smooth transition from EMT care to ACLS or hospital care is discussed.

The human heart is an elegantly designed and efficient pump that constantly responds to electrical, chemical, and mechanical stimuli during its normal operation. In an unhealthy heart, this balance of stimulus and response is disrupted. Because the *primary* stimulus of the human heart is electricity, electrical interventions are used to manage some cases of cardiac dysfunction.

This chapter focuses on the specific indications for and correct use of electrical countershock, including defibrillation and cardioversion. Cardiac pacing is also discussed.

Defibrillation

One of the most commonly used therapeutic interventions in the management of cardiac arrest is **defibrillation**. The defibrillator is used when a patient in sudden cardiac arrest is seen initially in ventricular fibrillation (VF), in pulseless ventricular tachycardia (VT), or fibrillates at some point during a call. Its purpose is to shock the heart back into a regular perfusing rhythm.

The concept behind defibrillation is simple. It is a countershock of electrical current, which is a sudden burst of electricity delivered by a defibrillator when the operator pushes the button. This countershock is

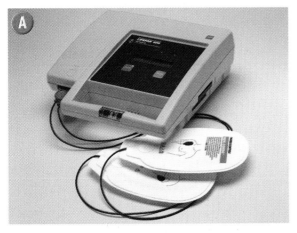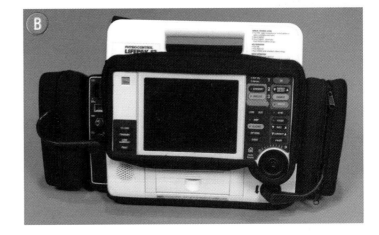

Figure 5-1 Two types of defibrillators. **A.** Automated. **B.** Manual.

intended to instantly depolarize the entire heart muscle simultaneously in hopes that the dysrhythmia will be terminated.

Once it has been determined that a shock is required, the operator pushes the button(s) and the defibrillator (**Figure 5-1**) generates and delivers electrical current. The current delivered usually ranges from 150 to 360 joules and is delivered to the patient's heart in a fraction of a second through the pads or paddles of the machine while on the patient's chest. If successful, when the countershock is applied, the heart's pumping action will become normal and result in a spontaneous return of pulse and blood pressure.

The defibrillator also is used when a patient presents in pulseless VT. It is noteworthy that VT in some patients produces a pulse and in other patients does not. Pulseless VT is treated exactly the same as VF.

VF is a chaotic rhythm with no discernible identifying features, such as P waves or QRS complexes. A random countershock, therefore, defibrillation, is the treatment of choice. Because there is no regular rhythm in VF, there is no way to coordinate the timing of the electrical pulse with any existing rhythm of the heart. The best response to VF or pulseless VT is a randomly applied countershock. (In this case, the word *randomly* means "at the discretion of the operator.")

> **O**ne of the most commonly used therapeutic interventions in the management of cardiac arrest is defibrillation.

defibrillation
The act of shocking a fibrillating (chaotically beating) heart with specialized electrical current in an attempt to restore a normal rhythm.

Training Tip

Take out the defibrillator used by your team and determine its type. How much time have you spent in training for its use?

> **T**he chances for recovery of heart rhythm by use of defibrillation decrease by approximately 10% for each minute the heart continues to fibrillate.

VF initially may be seen in 60% to 85% of patients in sudden cardiac arrest. When either VF or pulseless VT is present, the only effective treatment is defibrillation. CPR alone will not terminate VF or pulseless VT. Performing CPR, however, is vital to buy time until you can use the defibrillator. In these cases, CPR only extends the window of time in which defibrillation may be effective (**Figure 5-2**). Without defibrillation in patients with VF and pulseless VT, CPR only prolongs the act of dying.

Intervention	Survival Rate
Early defibrillation (6 minutes) with CPR and ALS	30%
Early defibrillation (6 minutes) with CPR	20%
Delayed defibrillation (10 minutes) with CPR	2% to 8%
Delayed defibrillation (10 minutes)	0% to 2%

Figure 5-2 CPR is vital to extending the time in which defibrillation may be effective for patients in VF or VT, but CPR alone will not correct the rhythm.

If a person in sudden cardiac arrest has prompt intervention, the likelihood of surviving neurologically intact—having no brain damage as a result of the cardiac arrest—has been documented at close to 90%. When compared with the current survival statistics for all victims of out-of-hospital sudden cardiac arrest (4% to 5%), that percentage is remarkable. Defibrillation works best if it takes place as soon as possible after the person arrests. Remember, to achieve better survival rates, seconds matter. However, it is important to note that automated external defibrillators (AEDs) should not be used on patients younger than age 8 years or who weigh less than 55 lb.

Another factor that has an impact on patient survival is continuity of care. Even if the patient can be shocked quickly into a perfusing rhythm, advanced cardiac care interventions often are required to keep the patient from refibrillating and to further stabilize the patient's condition.

According to the American Heart Association's guidelines, advanced cardiac care interventions include advanced airway management, drug therapy, or additional electrical interventions, such as cardiac pacing (discussed later in this chapter). Specific cardiac drug therapies will be discussed in Chapter 6, The Fundamentals of Cardiac Pharmacology.

Types of Defibrillators

Defibrillators are classified as either being manual or automated. The steps that must be performed by the operator vary greatly with each type of defibrillator.

Manual Defibrillators

In most EMS systems, EMT-Bs are not called on to perform **manual defibrillation**. However, as with other ACLS procedures, you may be called on to assist other providers with this skill. In operating a manual defibrillator (Table 5-1), the electrical countercharge is administered by placing the paddles correctly on the patient's body and holding them there for the defibrillation. In this situation, the provider performing manual defibrillation is in direct contact with the device at the point of shock delivery and holds the paddles during defibrillation.

manual defibrillation
A type of defibrillation in which the electrical countercharge is administered by placing the paddles on the patient's body and holding them there for defibrillation.

Table 5-1: Manual Defibrillation

Step	Operator Action Required
Turn defibrillator on	Yes
Confirm synchronizer is not on	Yes
Select energy level	Yes
Place/apply separate interface medium	Yes
Position the paddles	Yes
Charge the paddles	Yes
Clear the patient (visually/verbally)	Yes
Fire the defibrillator	Yes
Total operator steps/actions: 8	

Another way to defibrillate the patient manually is by administering the countercharge through monitoring pads already on the patient's chest. This option, often called "hands-free" defibrillation, actually is safer for the operator.

Manual defibrillators typically are used by physicians, nurses, and paramedics because of the additional options and features offered including the following:

- manual control of ECG size/display
- variable energy level choices
- cardioversion option
- "quick look" paddle capabilities

With these options comes a need for the operator to not only be well versed in the operation and multiple functions of the machine, but also to be able to analyze and identify a wide variety of cardiac rhythms. Attaining this knowledge requires a comprehensive initial education and training as well as continuing education in order to maintain competencies.

Automated Defibrillators

Semiautomated and automated defibrillators are both referred to as "automated." The steps necessary to operate the semiautomated and automated defibrillators are outlined in Tables 5-2 and 5-3. Implanted defibrillators are also discussed.

The simple design and ease of operation of semiautomated and fully automated defibrillators make these devices easier to operate than the manual defibrillator. The initial training required to operate a fully automated defibrillator is often no more than 2 or 3 hours and often includes a CPR review.

Safety During Defibrillation

One of the most hallowed rules of defibrillation is that the person pushing the button is ultimately responsible for safe operation of the defibrillator. Safe operation involves three separate yet related components. First, the patient must be confirmed to be pulseless, apneic, and in cardiac arrest. Second, the operator must be certain that he or she is personally clear of any patient contact. Third, it is essential to confirm that the other members of the rescue team also are clear of any contact with the patient. This third step is often one of the most difficult. If someone is trying to intubate or start an IV, he or she may be focusing so hard on the task that the directions to "stand back" are not heard. Therefore it is important to clear the team *verbally* and *visually* to make sure they are in fact clear prior to delivering the shock.

Automated Implantable Cardiac Defibrillators

Automated implantable cardiac defibrillators (AICDs) **(Figure 5-3)** usually are placed into patients with either a history of a near-death experience or who have been identified as having arrhythmias that are not suitably controlled with medications. When medication cannot provide

Table 5-2: Semiautomated Defibrillation

Step	Operator Action Required
Turn defibrillator on	Yes
Confirm synchronizer is off	No
Apply monitoring/ defibrillation pads	Yes
Select energy level	No
Place/apply separate interface medium	No
Position the paddles	No
Charge the defibrillator	Yes
Clear the patient (visually/verbally)	Yes
Fire the defibrillator	Yes
Total operator steps/actions: 5	

Table 5-3: Automated Defibrillation

Step	Operator Action Required
Turn defibrillator on	Yes
Confirm synchronizer is off	No
Apply monitoring/ defibrillation pads	Yes
Select energy level	No
Place/apply separate interface medium	No
Position the paddles	No
Charge the defibrillator	No
Clear the patient (visually/verbally)	Yes
Fire the defibrillator	No
Total operator steps/actions: 3	

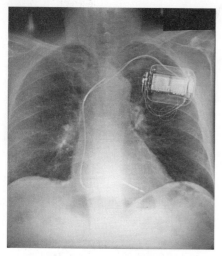

Figure 5-3 An automated implantable cardiac defibrillator (AICD) implanted into the chest.

| Box 5-1 | **Public Access Defibrillation Legislation** |

T he advent of automated defibrillators has made it possible for minimally trained or in some cases untrained nonmedical personnel to use a defibrillator on patients with sudden cardiac arrest prior to the arrival of the EMS team. The concept behind public access defibrillation (PAD) legislation is to make automated defibrillators easily accessible to the public so that anyone witnessing a sudden cardiac arrest can start defibrillation. PAD legislation has either been passed or is in the process of being passed across the United States.

In many cases, automated external defibrillator use is now included as an integral component of basic 8-hour first aid classes. Optimists see a point in the near future when AEDs will be available next to fire extinguishers. Again, it is hoped that by putting AEDs in places where the public has ready access to them, the time from a person's collapse into sudden cardiac arrest to defibrillation can be shortened further, increasing the number of survivors.

---

automated implantable cardiac defibrillator (AICD)
A defibrillator placed into patients with either a history of near-death experience or who have been identified as having arrhythmias that are not controlled suitably with medication.

T he primary focus in successful interventions with patients in sudden cardiac arrest is to reduce the time from collapse to the application of countershock.

adequate stabilization and the likelihood of having a near-death experience is high, an AICD is a life-or-death treatment option.

If a patient with an AICD is encountered and is in sudden cardiac arrest, resuscitation measures should still be implemented. If a cardiac monitor with a manual defibrillator is being used, the quick look paddles should be placed and the presenting rhythm identified. If the rhythm is shockable and the AICD is not firing, then standard protocol and defibrillation procedures should be followed. If your unit has an AED, it should be applied and the protocol for its use followed.

In either case, if the AICD is shocking a patient, expect a delay of about 60 seconds for it to complete its task. This time may vary depending on when you arrived on the scene; for example, the AICD may be halfway through its analysis/shock cycle. If 30 seconds pass with no response from the patient, implement the regular resuscitation protocol.

Another issue to keep in mind is that patients with AICDs are under tremendous emotional stress. To begin with, they have already been identified as being at high risk for sudden cardiac death. If that weren't the case, they probably wouldn't have an AICD.

In addition, if the AICD has previously discharged, the patient now exists in a state of emotional limbo, which adds to the stress level. The patient knows that each time the AICD discharges, the heart is in a possibly fatal rhythm. As you might imagine, this is not a comforting thought to live with daily. Given their increased stress level, a proportionate increase in empathy and sensitive communication is essential when treating these patients.

EMT-B Interventions

With the continuing expansion of AED use, there is greater likelihood that an EMT-B may provide the initial series of defibrillations to the patient in sudden cardiac arrest. Once the patient has been identified as being pulseless and apneic, immediate application of the AED and rapid defibrillation, if indicated, should occur. In addition, airway management, CPR, and requesting an ACLS response also are important aspects of the overall call management.

In some cases, you may have assumed care for the patient from citizen responders. In other cases, you may have initiated the primary care. Whatever the case, as long as the patient remains apneic and pulseless but not in a shockable rhythm, ongoing CPR in combination with the administration of high concentrations of oxygen and securing the airway by intubating may help to keep the patient viable and more responsive to ALS interventions.

Smooth Transition to ACLS Care

When ALS arrives, one potentially confusing aspect of the transition of care is what to do with the AED being used. Current recommendations from the American Heart Association state that if the AED is in place and has a screen to display the ECG, leave it in place for use by the ALS team. This instruction is given to limit the down time and interruptions in patient care caused by needless changes in equipment as leads and/or electrodes are removed and replaced.

If the AED in place does *not* show the ECG, the ALS team will need to apply their cardiac monitor/defibrillator. In this case, the best solution would be to use a simple adapter to connect the ALS team's monitor to the electrodes already placed on the patient by EMT-Bs for their AED.

Unfortunately, not all AEDs have the capability to use the simple adapter (**Figure 5-4**) to allow this smooth, efficient transfer of AEDs. The machines that don't allow the use of adapters take precious time away from the patient's care by requiring the removal of pads and leads and the reapplication of different pads for the ALS defibrillator.

Training Tip

Check to see if the monitoring electrodes used with your AED are compatible with the cardiac monitor used by any ALS service with whom you may work. If an adapter is needed, make certain that it is always stored with your AED and is clearly marked. Should more than one adapter be needed, as in the case in which multiple ALS providers are used, easy identification is a must.

If the electrodes used by your squad are going to be left in place, let the ALS team know that you are leaving the pads and disconnecting your AED. Get it out of the way so that the team can connect their monitor/defibrillator. If your electrodes need to be removed as well, remove them and wipe the skin area quickly under and around them with a

Figure 5-4 An AED adapter.

AUTOMATED EXTERNAL DEFIBRILLATOR
Daily/Shift Inspection Checklist

Serial # _____   Date _____   Time _____

Model # _____   Inspected by _____

Item	Pass	Fail
Exterior/Cables		
Nothing stored on top of unit		
Carry case intact and clean		
Exterior/LCD screen clean and undamaged		
Cables/connectors clean and undamaged		
Cables securely attached to unit		
Batteries		
Unit charger is plugged in and operational (if applicable)		
Fully charged battery in unit		
Fully charged spare battery		
Spare battery charger plugged in and operational (if applicable)		
Valid expiration date on both batteries		
Supplies		
Two sets of electrodes		
Electrodes in sealed packages with valid expiration dates		
Razor		
Hand towel		
Alcohol wipes		
Memory/voice recording device—module, card, microcassette		
Manual override—module, key (if applicable)		
Printer paper (if applicable)		
Operation		
Unit self-test per manufacturer's recommendation/instructions		
Display (if applicable)		
Visual indicators		
Verbal prompts		
Printer (if applicable)		
Attach AED to simulator/tester:		
Recognizes shockable rhythm		
Charges to correct energy level within manufacturer's specifications		
Delivers charge		
Recognizes nonshockable rhythm		
Manual override system in working order (if applicable)		

Signature

Figure 5-5 Sample AED daily checklist.

towel. This is an important step that serves a dual purpose. First, it dries the area in order to facilitate better contact for the next set of electrodes. Second, it will remove any residue from the interface medium that may remain from the other pads.

If any residue is left on the patient's chest, it may cause "bridging," a phenomenon that occurs when an electric current "jumps" from one defibrillation paddle to the other during defibrillation. Bridging is dangerous for the operator and the patient and must be avoided. This is because the full electric current does not penetrate the chest wall to reach the heart.

Once the ALS unit has taken over the defibrillation and your equipment is out of the way, there may be other ways you can assist the ALS team, including help with drug administration.

Defibrillator Care and Maintenance

Quite frequently, AEDs are the technology of choice for EMT-B squads because they are almost maintenance-free. Still, they are machines, and the possibility of mechanical failure, although small, exists.

Because of critical patient care implications in the event of an AED failure, each step should be taken to limit the likelihood of this occurring. One of the best ways to prevent AED failure is to follow the manufacturer's maintenance recommendations stringently, including the completion of any checklists provided to document any visual or physical checks to be routinely performed on the AED (**Figure 5-5**).

In the case of manual defibrillators, battery maintenance is one of the most important aspects of ensuring problem-free performance (**Figure 5-6**). Continued advances in battery technology have reduced the probability of battery failure. When battery failure does occur, it is more often than not linked to failure of personnel to adhere to battery care guidelines.

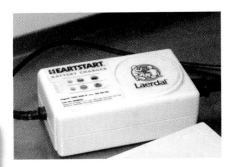

Figure 5-6 Battery maintenance is critical to an AED's performance.

Training Tip

Review your AED daily checklist and battery maintenance procedures in your EMT-B group.

Cardioversion

There are two primary types of electrical countershock used to treat various cardiac conditions. First is defibrillation, which we have discussed. Recall that it is a random countershock that is delivered when the operator presses the buttons to "fire" the defibrillator. **Cardioversion** also is a countershock, but in comparison, is a synchronized shock used to treat rhythms that still have all the components of a normal cardiac cycle, ie, a P wave, a QRS complex, and a T wave. During a cardioversion, the purpose of synchronizing the shock is to avoid delivering the shock and hitting the top of the T wave, which would, at least in theory, immediately put the patient in ventricular fibrillation resulting in cessation of pumping action.

cardioversion
A synchronized countershock used to treat rhythms that still have all the components of a normal cardiac cycle, ie, a P wave, a QRS complex, and a T wave. During a cardioversion, the purpose of synchronizing the shock is to avoid delivering the shock and hitting the top of the T wave, which would, at least in theory, immediately put the patient in ventricular fibrillation resulting in cessation of pumping action.

cardiac pacemaker
An electrical device that provides electrical pacing stimulus to a heart that is not pacing itself adequately.

Cardiac Pacing

Cardiac pacemakers, which were introduced in 1956, are used to manage slow heart rhythms or heart blocks, especially those not responding to conventional drug therapy. Although clearly innovative, pacemakers were used infrequently because of the pain they caused the patient each time one fired to stimulate the heart. Because the current was so high on these early pacemakers, patients received 70 or so painful shocks each minute and commonly were burned on their chest.

Over time, researchers learned that they could decrease the amount of current required by increasing the duration of the electric pulse. This welcome discovery greatly reduced the pain caused by the current. In addition, the pacing electrodes themselves were improved.

With today's pacing technology, especially with the minute amount of current being delivered (usually less than 100 milliamps), cardiac pacemakers pose little if any risk to EMTs. This also is true for someone performing CPR while the pacemaker is attempting to perform its pacing functions (**Figure 5-7**).

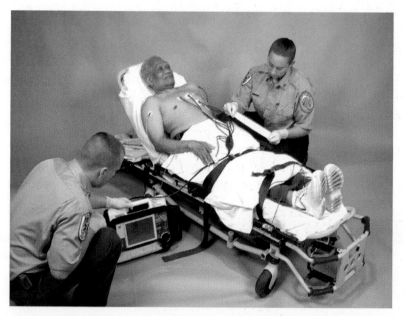

Figure 5-7 Patients may have implanted cardiac pacemakers. These pose little risk to emergency personnel and should not deter you from providing care.

Wrap Up

Ready for Review

Because of the key role that electrical therapy often plays in the care of the cardiac patient, it is essential that the EMT-B be knowledgeable of the principles and practices behind its use. This is beneficial in the areas of improving patient care as well as in the area of responder safety.

Quick Case

1. You and your partner are called to a residence for a man who cannot be awakened by his wife. When you arrive, you assess the man and find that he is pulseless and apneic. You attach the automated external defibrillator and initiate analysis of the patient's cardiac rhythm. It tells you that a "shock is advised."

   Why is it so important to deliver this shock immediately? By what percentage does this patient's chance for survival decrease if the shock is not delivered until 2 minutes later?

   _____

   _____

2. A 49-year-old man is complaining of pressure in his chest and nausea. After placing him on 100% oxygen, you begin to assess his vital signs. As you are taking his blood pressure, he suddenly loses consciousness. After determining that the patient is in cardiac arrest, you begin CPR as your partner runs to the ambulance to retrieve the automated external defibrillator.

   Assuming that this patient is in ventricular fibrillation, as are most patients with sudden cardiac arrest, why begin CPR if defibrillation is the most important therapy for this deadly rhythm?

   _____

   _____

3. Paramedics arrive on the scene where you and your partner are performing CPR on a man in cardiac arrest. Prior to ALS arrival, you delivered three defibrillations with your automated external defibrillator, which has a screen that displays the patient's cardiac rhythm.

   Why would the paramedic ask you to leave your AED in place if he or she has a manual defibrillator?

   _____

   _____

   _____

Chapter 6

The Fundamentals of Cardiac Pharmacology

C hemical or drug intervention is frequently utilized in emergency cardiac care. This chapter presents a list of the drugs most frequently used by ACLS teams in sudden cardiac arrest and other cardiac cases. Each drug description includes its proper name, its properties, and its specific effect on the body. After reading this chapter, you will have been exposed to the drug's uses, effects, most frequent dosages, and modes of delivery. As a result, you can positively affect patient outcomes as you work with ACLS teams.

This chapter on **cardiac pharmacology** is designed to be a practical summary of the drugs used in emergency cardiac care to provide you with core knowledge regarding the following:

- which drugs are commonly used in cardiac care
- the therapeutic benefits these key drugs are intended to provide
- which common side effects to stay alert for
- how each drug is usually administered

Cardiac drug therapy is focused on addressing specific problems. Because of that, most cardiac drugs fall into distinct categories. In general, they either speed the heart up, slow it down, make it less irritable, or make it more likely to respond to other therapies, such as defibrillation. Although some drugs have multiple functions, most are given for only one or two reasons.

Additional drugs discussed in this chapter are not necessarily specific to the heart, but are still used as adjunct therapies in cardiac care situations (**Figure 6-1**).

The EMT-B working in an ACLS environment requires only a basic knowledge of the drugs most commonly used to manage cardiac patients. Armed with this knowledge, you will know *what positive effects to expect* from certain drugs as well as *what to stay alert for* when certain drugs are being administered by ALS personnel.

EMT-Bs who have this basic knowledge of cardiac pharmacology will be an asset in the emergency situations they and the ACLS teams face every day. As most EMT-Bs know, many prehospital cardiac calls often have to be managed by a single paramedic or ALS provider working in harmony with one or two BLS providers. This means that all ALS tasks are performed by the paramedic or ALS provider and all other aspects of call management and supervision must be assumed by the EMT-B or other BLS personnel present.

The more trained and educated you are as an EMT-B working in the realm of ACLS, the better prepared you will be to anticipate needs and contribute to a positive outcome for the patient.

cardiac pharmacology
The study of drugs used in cardiac care and their therapeutic benefits, side effects, and administration.

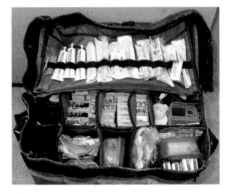

Figure 6-1 An ALS drug box.

> ### Training Tip
>
> After your next call with your ALS provider, find out the location of the primary drug box/jump kits. You also will want to know where to find the compartment where extra drugs are kept, for quick restocking when back-to-back calls keep the ambulance from returning to base for supplies.

> The EMT-B working in an ACLS environment requires only a basic knowledge of the drugs most commonly used to manage cardiac patients.

The Language of Pharmacology

Pharmacology is a specialized branch of medicine. Some important words and phrases that you will need to be familiar with include the following:

- <u>Indications</u> **for use**—The reason(s) a certain drug is administered to a patient.

- <u>Contraindications</u> **for use**—The reason(s) a certain drug should not be administered to a patient.

- <u>Therapeutic effects</u>—The positive, or desirable, effects expected to occur when a drug is administered.

- <u>Side effects</u>—Expected and predictable effects of a drug that are not part of the therapeutic effect.

- <u>Dosage</u>—The amount of drug required to produce the desired *therapeutic effect.* Dosage most often is stated in grams or portions of grams (for example, grams, milligrams, or micrograms) (**Figure 6-2**) because this denotes the actual *weight* of the drug. For each drug there is a *total allowable amount of drug that can be given to a patient within a certain time frame.* For example, 300 mg of lidocaine is the maximum amount normally given to an adult within 1 hour.

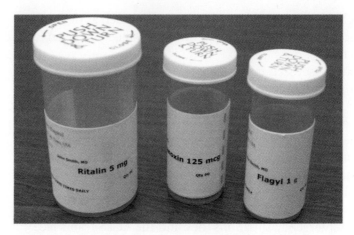

Figure 6-2 Dosage usually is stated in grams, milligrams, or micrograms.

- **Route of administration**—The method(s) by which a particular drug is given. Common routes include oral, inhalation, topical, and injection. In cardiac patients, most drugs are given intravenously (IV) because the drug reaches the heart more quickly. In the world of cardiac care, *time is muscle*—heart muscle that is! You don't want a part of your patient's heart to die because a pill takes 45 minutes to dissolve in the stomach when a drug could have been delivered to the heart through the bloodstream in seconds.

- **Inotropic**—Pertaining to the strength with which the heart contracts. If a drug is said to have a positive inotropic effect, it makes the heart beat stronger.

- **Chronotropic**—Pertaining to the rate or speed of the heart. If a drug has a positive chronotropic effect, it makes the heart rate speed up. A negative chronotrope does just the opposite; it slows the heart down.

- **Dromotropic**—Pertaining to the conduction of electricity.

Now that you have been exposed to some of the language of pharmacology, we can move to the part that is most useful for you as an EMT-B. Because administration of almost all cardiac drugs is outside the scope of practice of an EMT-B, you will be given practical, baseline knowledge of the drugs most commonly used in emergency cardiac care, why and how they are administered, and what you should watch for after they have been given.

Common Cardiac Drugs

Oxygen

Because it is part of our daily lives, it's easy to forget that **oxygen** is actually a drug. When atmospheric oxygen is inhaled 12 to 20 times each minute, it is not considered to be a drug. Oxygen is only one of the elements that exist naturally in the air we breathe. However, once you separate it from the air into a pure substance and place it in a green cylinder for a patient to inhale, it is considered to be a drug.

> **O**xygen is probably the most important drug in cardiac care, and you are the person who will administer it.

oxygen
A gas that cells need in order to metabolize; the heart and brain, especially, cannot function without oxygen.

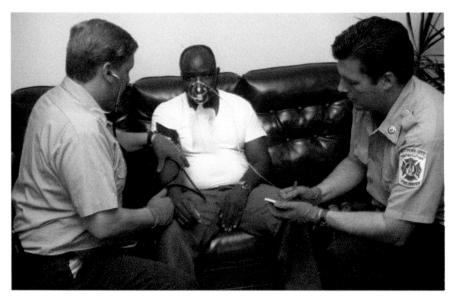

Figure 6-3 Administer high concentrations of oxygen to patients with acute chest pain or discomfort.

Oxygen therapy can help prevent some of the most dangerous and undesirable abnormal heart rhythms and is considered a key drug in the prevention of sudden cardiac arrest.

Oxygen is probably the most important drug in cardiac care, and is one drug received by all cardiac patients. Once the ALS team arrives, many patients are given epinephrine, while others may receive lidocaine. Still others are given morphine. However, *everyone* with a potential heart problem receives oxygen, and you may well be the person who starts the patient on this potentially life-saving therapy.

High concentrations of oxygen should be administered to any patient with acute chest pain or discomfort (**Figure 6-3**). Even if your patient does not use the word "pain," don't hesitate to use oxygen. Patients may say that their heart feels "funny" or "different" or that their chest "aches." Those terms and others like them point to cardiac problems, so don't ever withhold oxygen therapy from any patient whom you suspect may have a cardiac-related problem. When in doubt, administer oxygen.

Nitroglycerin

Along with oxygen, **nitroglycerin** is one of the most commonly used drugs in cardiac care. It has multiple uses, including the treatment of angina (exertional chest pain), heart attack, and left ventricular failure.

Nitroglycerin is a potent, fast-acting drug that can quickly relieve chest pain of cardiac origin. This smooth-muscle relaxant rapidly dilates the veins and coronary arteries. When coupled with oxygen therapy, nitroglycerin provides an effective treatment for relaxing blood vessels so that more oxygen gets to the ischemic heart.

Because of its potent **vasodilatory effects**, nitroglycerin can cause a patient's blood pressure to drop in a short time. The EMT-B should obtain a baseline blood pressure before the patient is given the drug. In

> **B**ecause nitroglycerin can cause a patient's blood pressure to drop quickly, causing a standing patient to fall, be sure the patient is lying down or seated safely when you administer the drug.

nitroglycerin
Medication that increases cardiac perfusion by blood flow by causing arteries to dilate; the EMT-B may be allowed to help the patient self-administer the medication.

vasodilatory effect
The widening of a blood vessel.

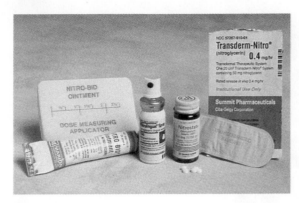

Figure 6-4 Nitroglycerin is one of the most commonly used drugs in cardiac care.

addition, remove all medication patches before administering multiple doses of nitroglycerin or other cardiac drugs.

Because nitroglycerin can cause a patient's blood pressure to drop quickly, causing a standing patient to fall, be sure the patient is lying down or seated safely when you administer the drug. Nitroglycerin is administered in the emergency setting either by a tablet under the tongue or by spray (**Figure 6-4**). Most patients get a pounding headache right after receiving this medication, so be prepared to tell them that this is normal and annoying but not a dangerous side effect.

You will want to remember that many patients who have had heart attacks may have their own supply of nitroglycerin and may have already placed one or two tablets under the tongue. Also, some patients wear nitroglycerin (nitro) patches, which provide a timed release of the medication. Be careful when you are removing the patches. Wipe clean any medication that gets on your skin, or you will have a pounding headache, too.

If severe chest pain is not relieved after three doses of nitroglycerin in 5-minute intervals, you may want to begin quietly setting up for a possible sudden cardiac arrest.

Keep in mind that the patient who has experienced previous serious damage to the heart as a result of an acute myocardial infarction (AMI) or massive heart attack actually may present in the early stages of heart failure, including pulmonary edema. A patient with pulmonary edema has difficulty breathing and needs to stay in a seated or semireclining position.

Because individuals with heart failure and acute pulmonary edema already have elevated blood pressure levels, nitroglycerin is not likely to drop their pressure to a dangerously low point.

> **A** patient with pulmonary edema has difficulty breathing and needs to stay in a seated or semi-reclining position.

epinephrine
A substance produced by the body (commonly called adrenaline), and a drug produced by pharmaceutical companies that increases pulse rate and blood pressure.

Epinephrine

Epinephrine (**Figure 6-5**) is the name for the laboratory-created version of the hormone adrenaline. We all make adrenaline naturally. It has many functions in survival, the most commonly known as the "fight or flight" response. Each of us can remember the surge of our own adrenaline when we barely escaped hitting another car or when we or someone we love was in a threatening situation. There was a surge of energy to our major muscles, our hearts, and our brains. It is this same immediate, powerful response that makes epinephrine so useful in cardiac medicine. This is especially true in sudden cardiac arrest management. The therapeutic effects of epinephrine include the following:

- increased blood pressure
- improved blood flow to the heart and brain
- increases in the strength of cardiac contraction (positive inotrope)
- increased likelihood of successful defibrillation
- increased electrical activity of the heart
- more effective CPR results

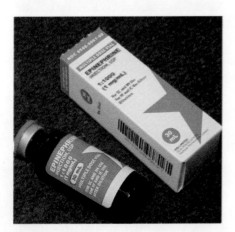

Figure 6-5 A multi-use vial of epinephrine.

Because of its systemic <u>**vasoconstrictive effects**</u>, epinephrine's primary benefit is improved perfusion of the heart and brain. Epinephrine is used for a variety of cardiac arrest rhythms. Under these circumstances, it is given every 3 to 5 minutes, with no dose limit as long as the patient is still pulseless. Epinephrine also occasionally is used for patients with very slow heart rates.

Potential Side Effects

Stay alert for an overly fast heart rate and a potential need to give the patient more oxygen. Keep in mind this basic equation for cardiac work: an increasing heart rate = an increased demand for oxygen. If the demand is not met, the heart malfunctions. Also, an increase in heart rate usually is followed by an increase in blood pressure. Blood pressures obtained frequently by the EMT-B can help ensure that the patient's condition doesn't deteriorate whenever epinephrine or another drug with positive chronotropic effects is given.

Vasopressin

<u>Vasopressin</u> (**Figure 6-6**) is a hormone that occurs naturally in the body, functioning primarily as an antidiuretic. In large doses, it becomes a potent vasoconstrictor that behaves much like epinephrine. Its use has gained favor because it does not increase cardiac ischemia or irritability, which may occur with epinephrine. Expect to see one dose of this drug used in a cardiac arrest where persistent ventricular fibrillation is a primary problem.

Adenosine

Like epinephrine, <u>adenosine</u> (**Figure 6-7**) also is a naturally occurring substance produced in the body. During the last few years, adenosine has gained wide acceptance in cardiac medicine. The main therapeutic effects of adenosine are that it slows conduction through the middle of the heart (the AV junction/AV node) and can almost instantly restore normal sinus rhythm in certain fast rhythms. One of the unique aspects of this drug is that once injected, the half-life of the drug is a matter of a few seconds!

Another important feature of adenosine is that when it is exerting its beneficial effect, there often is a period in which the heart presents in asystole. When this occurs, expect an asystole of 8 to 12 seconds or maybe longer. This can be unnerving for the novice provider watching a patient who just had a fast heart rate go into a phase where it looks like there is no heart beat! In the period of asystole, there is no electrical activity whatsoever appearing on the monitor. That brief period of flatline can seem like a lifetime!

Potential Side Effects

Because of its unique and fast mechanism of action, side effects with adenosine are common and include flushing, dyspnea, and, occasionally, chest pain. Given the rapid action and short half-life of the drug, most of the side effects go away quickly.

<u>**vasoconstrictive effect**</u>
The narrowing of a blood vessel, especially veins and arterioles of the skin.

<u>**vasopressin**</u>
A hormone that occurs naturally in the body, functioning primarily as an antidiuretic; becomes a potent vasoconstrictor in large doses.

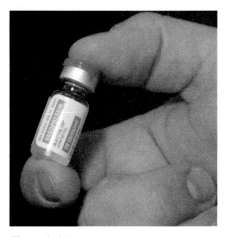

Figure 6-6 Vasopressin.

<u>**adenosine**</u>
A naturally occurring substance produced in the body; also used as a drug in cardiac medicine to slow conduction through the middle of the heart and restore normal sinus rhythm.

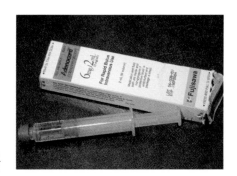

Figure 6-7 A box of adenosine.

> **A**nother important feature of adenosine is that when it is exerting its beneficial effect, there often is a period in which the heart presents in asystole.

lidocaine
An anesthetic drug used to raise the fibrillation threshold of the heart, suppress frequent premature ventricular contractions, and prevent repeat episodes of ventricular fibrillation.

Usual Dosage

Don't expect to see more than three doses of adenosine given to a patient. The initial 6-mg drug dose is followed by a 20-mL flush of normal saline, administered either by syringe or flushed from the IV bag. This saline "chaser" helps deliver the adenosine more quickly to the heart before the drug becomes inactive. If nothing happens within the next 1 or 2 minutes, the dose of adenosine is doubled to 12 mg and given again followed by 20 mL of normal saline by syringe or flushed from the IV bag. If there is still no response, it may be repeated once more at 12 mg. After that, another approach is taken.

Lidocaine

Lidocaine works primarily on the ventricles. Dentists use this synthetic anesthetic to numb the pain caused by drilling. Lidocaine also is used to lessen the pain of an irritable, hurting heart.

The main therapeutic effect of lidocaine is to raise the fibrillation threshold of the heart and therefore prevent repeat episodes of VF. Unfortunately, lidocaine usually doesn't help patients in VF who don't respond to defibrillation.

Although lidocaine is an anesthetic, it does not have a negative impact on the contraction of the heart or the patient's arterial blood pressure. These are desirable qualities because a heart with diminished pumping capabilities causes blood to back up into the lungs when the left ventricle cannot empty appropriately, resulting in acute pulmonary edema or congestive heart failure.

Expect to see lidocaine used as one of the drugs of choice after oxygen therapy when the ventricles begin to produce ectopic beats on their own. It also is frequently used for cardiac arrest patients who present in either VF or pulseless VT. (As pointed out in Chapter 5, although VF and pulseless VT are different cardiac rhythms, they usually are treated with the same approach, whether electrical or chemical.)

Lidocaine comes packaged in *two separate concentrations* (**Figure 6-8**). The 2% preparation is intended to be injected into the IV line as a single

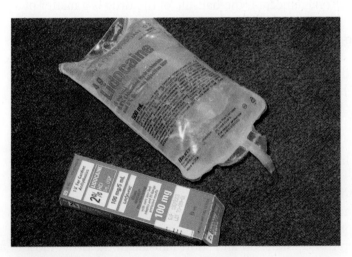

Figure 6-8 Premixed lidocaine used as a maintenance drip.

dose and is not mixed. The 20% solution is to be mixed into a bag of IV fluid then administered by IV piggyback so that the patient receives a continuous dose over an extended period of time. Although the packaging is clearly marked, it is good to understand the different doses and how they are administered.

Procainamide

Procainamide (**Figure 6-9**) is comparable in its actions to lidocaine and is used in similar situations. However, unlike lidocaine, procainamide must be administered slowly. Given the urgency of many cardiac emergencies, it makes sense that a drug that takes 4 or 5 minutes to administer is not a drug of first choice.

Expect procainamide to be used mainly for patients in VF or pulseless VT. When this drug is given to patients who have a pulse, procainamide has a potent vasodilatory effect in addition to decreasing the strength of the heart's contractions, so hypotension is the most common side effect. Careful monitoring of the blood pressure is indicated, and EMT-Bs can assist with this. Lastly, procainamide also slows conduction of electricity through the heart.

Amiodarone

This antiarrhythmic drug has continued to gain favor recently for use in emergency cardiac care, primarily in the setting of persistent or recurrent VF or pulseless VT. Expect to see one to two doses of **amiodarone** (**Figure 6-10**) given during a sudden cardiac arrest when the heart does not respond to multiple shocks.

Atropine

The main therapeutic effect of **atropine** is to increase the rate at which the heart paces itself by blocking parasympathetic stimulation to the sinoatrial (SA) node, the primary pacemaker of the heart (**Figure 6-11**). It also improves conduction (positive dromotrope) through the tissue in

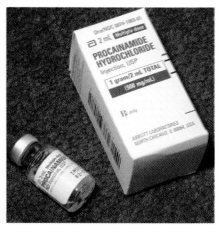

Figure 6-9 A multi-use vial of procainamide.

procainamide
A drug similar in its actions to lidocaine, but that must be administered slowly, thereby not making it the drug of first choice in many cardiac emergencies.

amiodarone
An antiarrhythmic drug given during sudden cardiac arrest when the heart does not respond to multiple shocks.

atropine
A drug that increases the rate at which the heart paces itself by blocking parasympathetic stimulation to the sinoatrial (SA) node. This drug is used for patients with symptomatic bradycardia or other conduction problems.

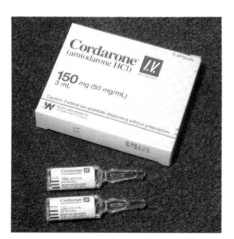

Figure 6-10 Amiodarone.

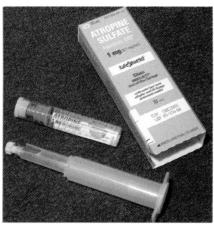

Figure 6-11 A box of preload atropine.

the middle of the heart located between the atria and ventricles, for example, the atrioventricular (AV) node.

Expect to see atropine used for patients with symptomatic bradycardia (a pulse of less than 60 beats/min with hypotension) or conduction problems, such as for some heart blocks.

A heart block is a condition in which an electrical impulse generated by the primary pacemaker of the heart, the SA node, fails to conduct down through the atria to the ventricles. For each of these blocked impulses and "lost" contractions, a drop in blood pressure occurs. If enough of these impulses are blocked, blood pressure can drop too far too fast and the patient will die. Atropine is given to improve conductivity so that electrical impulses reach the nonfiring muscles.

Dosage

Atropine is a potent drug given in several small doses, up to a total of 3 mg.

Potential Side Effects

An EMT-B can help monitor the patient's heart rate to ensure that the atropine doesn't increase the heart rate too much.

One important warning about the administration of atropine is that it must be injected quickly into the IV line. If atropine is given too slowly, it slows the heart rate even further. (This is called a paradoxical effect.) Therefore, monitoring the patient's blood pressure is an important part of your responsibility.

You also may see atropine given to patients in asystole. Recall that asystole often is referred to as flatline, which is what shows on the ECG monitor when the heart has no electrical activity. Given what you know at this point, once an adult heart is in flatline, there is very little chance that the patient can be successfully resuscitated unless atropine has been administered to the patient and electrical activity results.

Magnesium

<u>Magnesium</u> (**Figure 6-12**) is a naturally occurring electrolyte found in the body. Its primary therapeutic effect is its action as a central nervous system depressant. When the body has inadequate magnesium levels, it is common to see a high frequency of undesirable cardiac rhythms and possibly even cardiac arrest. For patients in VF, low levels of magnesium (hypomagnesia) can cause the heart to become unresponsive, or refractory (resistant), to conventional therapies. IV administration of magnesium reduces the frequency of complications for heart attack patients. It also seems to keep patients from experiencing VT or VF and, as such, reduces the likelihood of sudden cardiac arrest. Magnesium also is used in the treatment of an unusual form of ventricular tachycardia called **torsade de pointes**.

In spite of these desirable therapeutic effects, not enough data currently exist to move magnesium into a first-line position in prehospital medicine. As such, it remains in the drug boxes in some EMS systems.

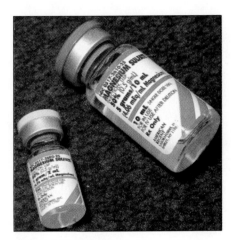

Figure 6-12 Magnesium.

magnesium
A naturally occurring electrolyte in the body; as a drug, it depresses the central nervous system, which may be useful in managing some cases of ventricular fibrillation in which the patient is resistant to conventional therapies.

torsade de pointes
An undulating sinusoidal rhythm in which the axis of the QRS complexes changes from positive to negative and back in a haphazard fashion.

Morphine

Chest pain and increased anxiety are common signs and symptoms in cardiac patients. Collectively, they push patients further into the "fight or flight" mode with the resulting increase in cardiac workload—an undesirable situation for a malfunctioning or damaged heart. Because of its potent analgesic effects, **morphine** is the drug of choice when rapid anxiety adjustment and pain management are desired. This drug also has limited vasodilatory effects, which helps reduce preload to the heart (**Figure 6-13**).

morphine
An analgesic drug of choice when rapid anxiety adjustment and pain management are desired.

Potential Side Effects

Morphine is classified as a narcotic, which causes central nervous system depression. With that comes respiratory depression—one of its most worrisome side effects. It is important to be alert for hypotension and the possibility of central nervous system depression, nausea, and vomiting.

Dosage

Because of CNS depression, expect to see morphine given in multiple small doses, usually 2 to 5 mg each. The maximum dosage allowed depends on local protocol. If too much morphine is administered and the patient becomes overly hypotensive, naloxone (Narcan) can be given in a dosage of 0.4 to 2.0 mg to reverse the effects instantly. Although this quick turnaround reverses the hypotension, expect the anxiety and chest pain to come back as well.

Nitrous Oxide

The use of nitrous oxide to control pain and anxiety in the cardiac patient (**Figure 6-14**) is unique when compared to most other drugs we have discussed in that it is *self-administered by the patient.*

Nitrous oxide is an inhaled gas that usually is administered in a 50/50 concentration of oxygen and nitrous oxide. Patients hold the mask to their face and breathe in, usually receiving pain relief in about 1 to 2 minutes. If too much nitrous oxide is inhaled, they may become drowsy and drop the mask, causing the effects of the nitrous oxide to quickly

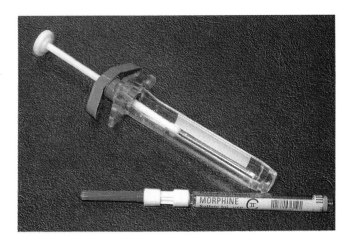

Figure 6-13 Morphine.

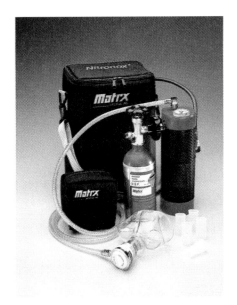

Figure 6-14 A nitronox unit.

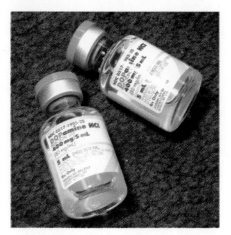

Figure 6-15 Dopamine.

dopamine

An inotropic drug most commonly used to raise a patient's blood pressure, usually administered by IV piggyback, and whose effects are dose dependent.

wear off. The ALS team may ask you to explain the use of nitrous oxide to the patient before it is administered, while the ACLS team continues with other procedures or drug therapies.

Dopamine

One of the most unique agents found in the cardiac care drug box is **dopamine** (**Figure 6-15**). This selective inotropic agent/vasopressor is most commonly used to raise a patient's blood pressure.

Dosage and Delivery

Dopamine is usually added to a bag of IV fluid and administered by IV piggyback, allowing for continuous administration of the drug in the dose range indicated.

Important Note

The effects of dopamine on the cardiovascular system are *dose dependent,* which means that its effects are markedly different at different doses.

When given at low doses, dopamine improves blood flow to the brain, kidneys, and the mesentery. As the dosage is increased, dopamine begins to constrict the vasculature and increases cardiac output, which combine to raise blood pressure even further. In situations in which the blood pressure remains inadequate, a high dose of dopamine is given. Although this provides a quick, marked improvement in blood pressure, the kidneys are adversely affected and potentially damaged.

As with some other drugs, dopamine increases the workload of the heart. However, the need to maintain adequate perfusion pressure takes precedence in this situation.

Indications

Expect to see dopamine used mainly for patients in cardiogenic shock, a life-threatening cardiac situation. A possible indicator of cardiogenic shock is an elevated heart rate, usually greater than 110 or 120 beats/min, and a low blood pressure, with a systolic blood pressure in the 60 mm Hg range or lower. When this mismatch of heart rate and blood pressure occurs in the context of a heart attack, cardiogenic shock often is the cause.

When a patient's blood pressure needs to be raised, the treatment choices include adding fluids or constricting the blood vessels. The EMT-B can help by keeping a close watch on lung sounds that may indicate fluid overload.

isotonic crystalloids

The main type of fluid used in the prehospital setting for fluid replacement because of its ability to support blood pressure by remaining within the vascular compartment.

access port

A sealed hub on an administration set designed for sterile access to the fluid.

administration set

Tubing that connects to the IV bag access port and the catheter in order to deliver the IV fluid.

piercing spike

The hard, sharpened plastic spike on the end of the administration set designed to pierce the sterile membrane of the IV bag.

> ### Training Tip
>
> Ask your ALS provider agency to save the drug boxes after the next code in order to familiarize yourself with what they look like. This will make them easier to locate if you are asked to assist with a particular drug.

Intravenous Therapy

In administering intravenous (IV) therapy, teamwork between BLS and ALS providers is critical. Given the time-sensitive nature of cardiac calls, your role in helping the patient receive IV therapy as quickly and smoothly as possible could contribute to making the call a success. Now that you have learned about various cardiac drugs, you will learn the steps for preparing a patient for IV therapy.

Choosing an IV Solution

In the prehospital setting, the choice of IV solution is usually limited to the <u>isotonic crystalloids</u> normal saline and lactated Ringer's solution. D_5W (5% dextrose in water) may also be administered, but is often reserved for administering medication because the presence of dextrose has the potential to alter fluid and electrolyte levels in the body.

Each IV solution bag is wrapped in a protective sterile plastic bag and keeping it sterile until the posted expiration date. Once the protective wrap is torn and removed, the IV solution has a shelf life of 24 hours. The bottom of each IV bag has two ports: an injection port for medication, and an <u>access port</u> for connecting the administration set. The sterile access port is protected by a removable cover that represents a point-of-no-return line—once this cover is removed, the bag must be used immediately or discarded.

IV solution bags come in different fluid volumes (**Figure 6-16**). Volumes commonly used in hospitals are 1,000 mL, 500 mL, 250 mL, and 100 mL; the more common prehospital volumes are 1,000 mL, 500 mL, and 250 mL.

Choosing an Administration Set

An <u>administration set</u> allows the fluid to move from the IV bag into the patient's vascular system. As with IV solution bags, IV administration sets are sterile as long as they remain in their protective packaging. Once they are removed from the packaging, their sterility cannot be guaranteed. Each IV administration set has a <u>piercing spike</u> protected by a plastic cover. Again, once the piercing spike is exposed and the seal surrounding the cap is broken, the set must be used immediately or discarded.

There are different sizes of administration sets for different situations and patients. **Drip sets** have a number visible on the package (**Figure 6-17**), which indicates the number of drops it takes for a milliliter of fluid to pass through the orifice and into the <u>drip chamber.</u> Drip sets come in two primary sizes: microdrip and macrodrip. **Microdrip sets** allow 60 <u>gtt</u> (drops)/mL through the small, needlelike orifice inside the drip chamber. Microdrips are ideal for medication administration or pediatric fluid delivery because it is easy to control their fluid flow. <u>Macrodrip sets</u> allow 10 to 15 gtt/mL through a large opening between the piercing spike and the drip chamber. Macrodrip sets are best used for rapid fluid replacement but can also be used for maintenance and <u>keep-the-vein-open (KVO) IV set-ups</u>.

Preparing an Administration Set

After choosing the IV administration set and the IV solution bag, verify the expiration date of the solution and check for solution clarity. Prepare to spike the bag with the administration set as indicated in *Skill Drill 6-1*.

Most, if not all, cardiac patients will need IV access should they have an immediate need for medications. The EMT-B's work to quickly establish a patent IV line will positively impact the outcome of the call.

Figure 6-16 Examples of different IV bag sizes.

<u>drip set</u>
Another name for an administration set.

<u>drip chamber</u>
The area on the administration set where fluid accumulates so that the tubing remains filled with fluid.

<u>microdrip set</u>
An administration set named for the small orifice between the piercing spike and the drip chamber. A microdrip set allows for carefully controlled fluid flow and is ideally suited for medication administration.

<u>gtt</u>
A measurement that indicates drops per milliliter.

<u>macrodrip set</u>
An administration set named for the large orifice between the piercing spike and the drip chamber. A macrodrip set allows for rapid fluid flow into the vascular system.

<u>keep-the-vein-open (KVO) IV set-up</u>
A phrase that refers to the flow rate of a maintenance IV line established as a prophylactic access.

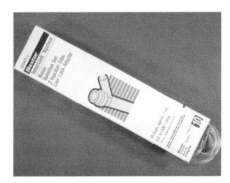

Figure 6-17 The number visible on the drip set refers to the number of drops it takes for a milliliter of fluid to pass through the orifice and into the drip chamber.

Skill Drill 6-1 Spiking the Bag

Remove the rubber cover found on the end of the IV bag by pulling on it. The bag is still sealed and will not leak until the piercing spike of the IV punctures this port.

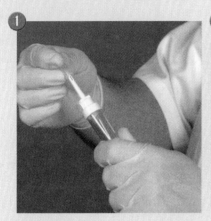

1

Remove the protective cover from the piercing spike (remember, this spike is sterile!).

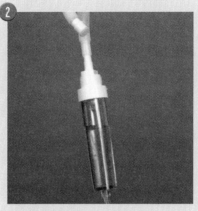

2

Slide the spike into the IV bag port and gently squeeze the drip chamber once or twice until it is half full.

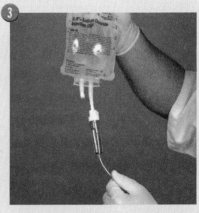

3

Allow the solution to run freely through the drip chamber and into the tubing to prime the line and flush the air out of the tubing.

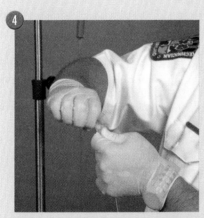

4

Twist the protective cover on the opposite end of the IV tubing to allow air to escape. Do not remove this cover yet, because the cover keeps the tubing end sterile until it is needed. Let the fluid flow until air bubbles are removed from the line before turning the roller clamp wheel to stop the flow.

5

Next, go back and check the drip chamber; it should be only half filled. The fluid level must be visible to calculate drip rates. If the fluid level is too low, squeeze the chamber until it fills; if the chamber is too full, invert the bag and the chamber and squeeze the chamber to force some fluid back into the bag.

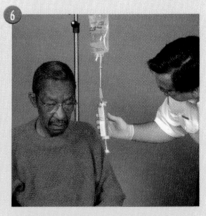

6

Hang the bag in an appropriate location with the end of the IV tubing easily accessible.

Wrap Up

Chapter 6
The Fundamentals of Cardiac Pharmacology

Ready for Review

Since administration of almost all cardiac drugs is outside the scope of practice of an EMT-B, a practical, baseline knowledge of the drugs most commonly used in emergency cardiac care, why they are administered, and how they are administered is important. You should now know what to watch for and how to assist ACLS providers after each of these drugs has been given.

You should be familiar with drug uses, effects, and most frequent dosages and modes of delivery. With this knowledge, you will be able to assist ACLS teams, and together you can help save the lives of patients in sudden cardiac arrest.

Quick Case

1. A middle-aged man is complaining of severe chest pain that radiates to his left arm and jaw. His blood pressure is 150/90 mm Hg, and his pulse is 110 beats/min. You have just finished assisting the paramedic in initiating an intravenous line. Medical control has ordered the paramedic to administer morphine to this patient by the intravenous route.

   Why is it more beneficial to the patient to give this drug intravenously as opposed to direct injection into the muscle of the patient's upper arm? What potential side effects should you be alert for after the administration of this particular drug?

   _____

   _____

   _____

   _____

   _____

2. You request an ALS ambulance to respond to the scene of a patient complaining of chest pain. Your rationale for this request was due to the fact that the patient's blood pressure was 70/40 mm Hg, and his heart rate was 140 beats/min. When the paramedics arrive, they assess the patient and decide to administer dopamine, which is an inotropic vasopressor drug.

   Through what effect will an inotropic drug raise this patient's blood pressure? Why would the paramedic *not* administer a chronotropic drug?

   _____

   _____

   _____

   _____

   _____

3 While you provide care to a 59-year-old woman with chest pain, she tells you that she took two of her prescribed nitroglycerin tablets prior to your arrival, but her pain has only improved minimally. You contact medical control and are advised to assist the patient with one more of her nitroglycerin tablets and then assess her blood pressure.

What are the therapeutic effects of nitroglycerin in relieving chest pain of cardiac origin? What is medical control's rationale for asking you to obtain another blood pressure reading after administering the third nitroglycerin?

_____

_____

_____

_____

_____

4 After performing defibrillation on a patient in cardiac arrest, the paramedic asks you to resume CPR. After establishing an intravenous line, the drug epinephrine is administered.

Through what effect(s) will this drug enhance the effectiveness of the CPR that you are performing?

_____

_____

_____

_____

_____

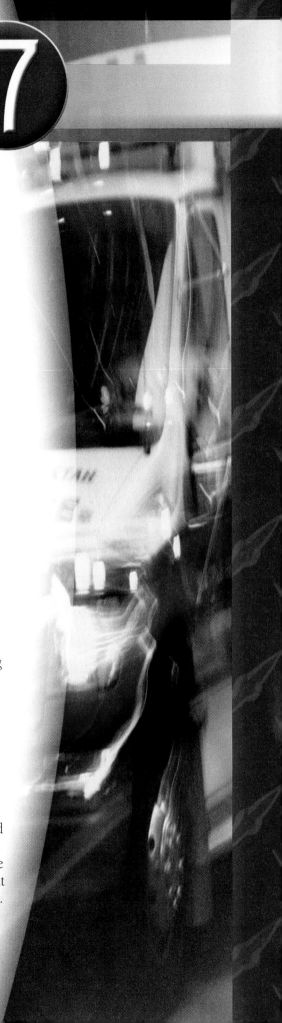

Chapter 7

Challenging Resuscitation Situations

T This chapter presents several of the most challenging resuscitation situations you will encounter, including stroke, electrical shock, lightning strikes, and large accident scenes. You will learn how to assess a stroke patient using two different scales, the Glasgow Coma Scale and the Cincinnati Stroke Scale. Drug-related cardiac emergencies are described, and the effects on patients produced by overdoses of both legal and illegal drugs are explained.

Few if any prehospital calls follow clinical or textbook presentations anywhere close to 100%. This chapter presents a number of challenging resuscitation situations that EMT-Bs may encounter, along with recommendations as to how they might best contribute to ALS patient care efforts.

Stroke or Brain Attacks

For years, <u>**cerebrovascular accident (CVA)**</u> was the term used to describe the condition resulting from decreased oxygen delivery to the brain, resulting in cerebral ischemia. In some cases, the CVA was caused by a blockage in the artery or reduction in blood flow, while in other cases, the culprit was a hemorrhage inside or around the brain itself. We now know that this medical event is by no means an accident. To a great extent it is a predictable event and, to a lesser degree, a preventable one. As a result, this event is now called a stroke or brain attack.

cerebrovascular accident (CVA)
An interruption of blood flow to the brain that results in the loss of brain function; also called stroke or brain attack.

In the past, a stroke patient was treated as a nonemergent patient, suggesting that the damage was present and irreversible. Because there was no hope of correcting the damage, there was little to be done other than to provide routine transport to the hospital emergency department (ED) to confirm the diagnosis and plan for the patient's long-term care. Recent advances in stroke treatment have caused a radical change in perceptions. Now, people know that if this often-catastrophic event is quickly recognized and treatment is started early enough after symptom onset, permanent damage can be avoided or reduced. This is especially encouraging news given the magnitude of the problem.

Stroke is the third leading cause of death in the United States in adults and is the leading cause of long-term disability (Table 7-1). Approximately 500,000 Americans will have a stroke this year. For many, it will be a first-time occurrence. For others, it will be a recurrent event. Collectively, about 150,000 of these individuals will die. Given the absence of treatment options in the past, those who did survive often fared poorly from this profoundly life-changing event. Many were left unable to walk or communicate effectively, while others were left unable to even feed or provide basic care for themselves.

It is hoped that this sad history will not be part of the future. The use of thrombolytics for the first time have offered medical practitioners a tool to reduce or reverse the neurologic insult frequently incurred by stroke patients. Research continues in the area of neuroprotective agents—another exciting and still emerging therapy. These agents may one day contribute to reducing mortality and morbidity even further.

As mentioned previously, the neurologic impairment resulting from a stroke is the result of two different mechanisms (**Figure 7-1**). <u>Ischemic</u>

Table 7-1: Leading Causes of Death in the United States, Year 2000

- Heart disease
- Cancer
- Stroke
- Chronic lower respiratory disease
- Accidents
- Diabetes
- Pneumonia/influenza
- Alzheimer's disease
- Nephritis, nephrotic syndrome, or nephrosis
- Septicemia

Source: National Vital Statistics Report, Vol. 49, No. 12.

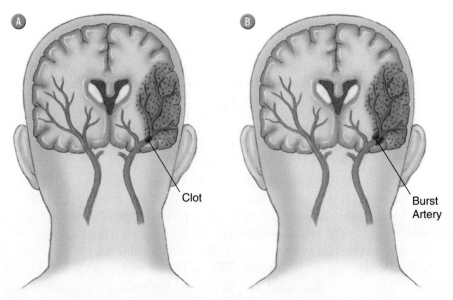

Clot

Burst Artery

Figure 7-1 Neurologic impairment caused by stroke results from one of two different mechanisms: ischemic stroke **(A)** or hemorrhagic stroke **(B)**.

strokes result from the disruption of blood flow because of the partial or complete occlusion of a blood vessel supplying the brain. Roughly three out of four strokes are in this category, commonly as a result of blood clots that develop within a blood vessel in the brain (**cerebral thrombosis**). The disruption also could result from clots that originated elsewhere in the body but moved through the cardiovascular system before finally causing a blockage in the brain (**cerebral embolism**). **Hemorrhagic strokes** are caused by disruption of blood flow as well, but in this case the precipitating event is the rupture of a cerebral artery, either above the surface of the brain or within the brain. Frequently, this event occurs as a by-product of hypertension.

Risk Factors for Stroke

The most effective and certainly least costly approach to stroke is prevention, rather than trying to correct or repair the damage produced by a stroke.

Although some strokes occur without symptoms or warning, it usually is the exception rather than the rule. The predictors, or what might better be termed risk factors, for stroke have been identified and categorized as being either controllable or uncontrollable (Table 7-2). Those that are classified as controllable should either be eliminated or treated as much as possible, although genetics plays a role in these factors to some extent. By comparison, nothing can be done to diminish uncontrollable risk factors.

The Events Leading Up to a Stroke

Most strokes do not occur without warning. They are preceded by a series of **transient ischemic attacks (TIAs)**. A TIA is a neurologic deficit resulting from a brain ischemia whose symptoms resolve within 24 hours. The EMT-B can play a key role if the signs and symptoms of a TIA are recognized. However, these signs and symptoms can be subtle and transient, which increases the difficulty of prompt recognition. With more training and education, recognition and care of TIAs in the field setting will improve.

Studies have shown that **tissue plasminogen activator (tPA)** improves neurologic outcomes if given to patients with ischemic stroke within 3 hours of symptom onset. Ideally, when a stroke patient is recognized in the field, a call can be made to alert the ED so thrombolytic therapy can be initiated on arrival at the hospital.

ischemic stroke
One of the two main types of stroke; occurs when blood flow to a particular part of the brain is cut off by a blockage (eg, a clot) inside a blood vessel.

cerebral thrombosis
A clot in the brain that results in a blockage called a cerebral embolism.

cerebral embolism
Obstruction of a cerebral artery caused by a clot that was formed elsewhere in the body and traveled to the brain.

hemorrhagic stroke
One of the two main types of stroke; occurs as a result of bleeding inside the brain.

Table 7-2: Risk Factors for Stroke

Controllable Risk Factors
- Hypertension
- Heart disease
- Elevated cholesterol levels
- Diabetes
- Tobacco use
- Alcohol use
- Obesity
- Inactive lifestyle

Uncontrollable Risk Factors
- Age > 55 years
- Male gender
- Race
- Heredity
- Previous stroke

transient ischemic attack (TIA)
A disorder of the brain in which brain cells temporarily stop working because of insufficient oxygen, causing stroke-like symptoms that resolve completely within 24 hours of onset.

tissue plasminogen activator (tPA)
A drug that improves neurologic outcomes if given to patients with ischemic stroke within 3 hours of symptom onset.

Training Tip

Make arrangements to observe stroke patients at a local rehabilitation facility. You will be able to see the various ways strokes can cause damage. Contact your local or state EMS authority to see if you can obtain continuing education credit toward your recertification.

Prehospital Care of the Stroke Patient

The good news is that you can help stroke patients survive until they arrive at the hospital. Most of the initial prehospital care commonly required by stroke patients falls within the scope of practice of EMT-Bs.

Airway obstruction can result from paralysis of the muscles of the face, throat, tongue, and mouth. If positioning alone is not effective in maintaining an open airway, use of an oropharyngeal airway or a nasopharyngeal airway may be indicated. Suction should be set up and ready to remove saliva or vomit to reduce the risk of aspiration.

Oxygen therapy may be beneficial and should be initiated promptly. A nasal cannula, while not providing a high concentration of oxygen, allows easier access for suctioning than various mask-style oxygen delivery devices. However, if the patient needs a higher concentration of oxygen than a nasal cannula will deliver, an adjunct, such as a nonrebreathing mask, should be used.

In the event that a traumatic event, such as a fall or car crash, may have accompanied the stroke, measures to restrict spinal motion may be indicated. Whenever possible, place the patient in a neutral position, place a rigid cervical collar, and use care when logrolling the patient onto the backboard or when placing the patient in the recovery position.

Be alert for abnormal respiratory patterns such as Cheyne-Stokes or central neurogenic hyperventilation. Hypoventilation from shallow respirations or poor air exchange also can be a concern. You may gain even more valuable insights by using the Cincinnati Stroke Scale (Table 7-3). Stroke patients requiring rescue breathing for respiratory arrest secondary to their cerebral event should not be expected to have a positive outcome, irrespective of the patient care interventions provided.

Of course, some stroke patients require ALS interventions to supplement the initial BLS care. You can be helpful in making the call to request ALS. Stroke patients who initially are seen comatose (**Glasgow Coma Scale** score of 8 or less) are good candidates for endotracheal intubation as a preventive measure. Intubation can be performed by the EMT-B in some EMS systems. In systems where this still is not allowed, however, the EMT-B can assist the paramedic or other ALS provider during intubation.

Glasgow Coma Scale
A method of evaluating level of consciousness that uses a scoring system for neurologic responses to specific stimuli.

Table 7-3: The Cincinnati Stroke Scale

What to Look For	How to Evaluate	Normal	Abnormal
Facial Droop	Ask the patient to smile or show you his or her teeth.	Face is symmetric and both sides move equally well.	Asymmetry and/or unequal facial movements.
Arm Drift	Have the patient close his or her eyes and hold the arms out.	Both arms remain still or move the same.	One arm drifts down or does not move.
Speech	Ask the patient to say "You can't teach an old dog new tricks."	Patient uses correct words with no slurring.	Patient can't speak, slurs words, or uses inappropriate words.

In addition, cardiovascular complications are common in the context of stroke. There are some cases in which a cardiac condition may have caused the stroke, as in the case of blood clots forming as a result of atrial fibrillation. With this particular rhythm, the top two receiving chambers of the heart (the atria) fibrillate, or quiver uncontrollably, without producing effective pumping action. When this happens, the blood moves sporadically into the ventricles, occasionally sitting long enough for clots to start forming. There also is an estimated 25% drop in cardiac output when atrial fibrillation occurs. This cardiac rhythm is infrequently treated in the field setting unless the ventricular response is greater than 100 and produces hypotension and an unstable condition. When cardiac events are associated with a stroke, careful monitoring of the patient's blood pressure and cardiac rhythm always is a good idea.

Another ALS intervention indicated is intravenous (IV) access. A saline lock (also called a buff cap) usually will suffice, because fluid resuscitation is rarely indicated for these patients, so the point of the IV access is for drug administration purposes. Drug therapy may be required for seizure control or treatment of hypoglycemia or arrhythmia. If IV fluids are administered, isotonic fluids are the fluids of choice and should be run at either "to keep open" (TKO) rates or less than 30 mL/h, unless hypovolemia is identified as a problem.

Trauma-induced Cardiac Arrest

Cardiac arrest that occurs secondary to trauma is a grave event associated with poor outcomes. The most common traumatic causes/mechanisms include:

- Airway obstruction
- Devastating head trauma
- Massive blood loss
- Great vessel damage
- Extensive damage directly to the heart
- Tension pneumothorax
- Cardiac tamponade

Given the extent and severity of body damage represented by these mechanisms, the dismal survival numbers come as no surprise. Poor survival, however, does not imply that the EMT-B should give up and do nothing for the patient. To put this challenging situation in perspective, let's back up and work through the process.

When an EMT-B unit is dispatched to a serious trauma scene or event as identified by the caller (especially if it was called in by law enforcement), a request for ALS should be made immediately (**Figure 7-2**). If a helicopter routinely transports seriously injured patients to a local trauma center, contact the center and put personnel on standby. This will allow the flight team to start the preflight routine, evaluate weather conditions, and identify the most appropriate landing zone near the emergency scene.

If patients have been determined to be in cardiac arrest prior to your arrival at the emergency scene, don't consider this an indisputable fact.

Figure 7-2 When dispatched to a serious trauma scene, request ALS immediately.

An injured patient with extensive blood loss may have a very fast, weak pulse that was overlooked by the person who made the determination. The person also may have checked a radial pulse, which, given a number of severe injuries or condition, may not be present. In some cases, a carotid pulse may still be palpable but may not have been checked. This also could lead to the erroneous assumption that the patient is in trauma-induced cardiac arrest. Don't take for granted that any patient is in cardiac arrest unless identified as such by an EMS professional.

Again, make certain that ALS is en route. If they have not already been requested, call them immediately. Keep in mind that it is better to request ALS and not need them than to have a patient suddenly turn critical and need ALS interventions only to find out that ALS is not on scene, or worse yet, not en route.

Some of the common causes of trauma-induced cardiac arrest and the corresponding EMT-B interventions include those listed in **Table 7-4**. For patients who are seen in cardiac arrest but do not have obvious signs of serious trauma, the cardiac event may have preceded the traumatic event. In this case, apply an AED, if one is available. If the patient is in ventricular fibrillation, rapid defibrillation may be successful. If the patient is in ventricular fibrillation secondary to blood loss and the fluid and electrolyte imbalance that results, electrical therapy in the form of defibrillation will not solve the problem.

Any other conditions identified as being correctable or controllable should be addressed by the EMT-B, because these may result in a successful resuscitation or prevent cardiac arrest from occurring.

> **K**eep in mind that it is better to request ALS and not need them than to have a patient suddenly turn critical and need ALS interventions, only to find out that ALS is not on scene or, worse yet, not en route.

Hypothermia

hypothermia
A condition in which the internal body temperature falls below 95°F (35°C), usually as a result of prolonged exposure to cool or freezing temperatures.

Whenever a person's body temperature drops below 95°F, the condition is known as **hypothermia**. Hypothermia can occur suddenly—for example, by submersion in freezing water after a fall through ice. In a scenario such as this, the person can become mentally and physically incapacitated in just a few minutes. By comparison, an elderly person who falls to a cold tile floor, fractures a hip, and then lies there for several hours also can become hypothermic. Although these situations are distinctly different, each can produce a similar result.

Regardless of the mechanism, as the body's core temperature begins to fall, normal body functions begin to falter. A core temperature of 95°F to 86°F would be classified as mild hypothermia. Once the core temperature dips below 86°F, cardiac output falls, blood pressure drops, and blood flow to the brain decreases. This is classified as severe hypothermia. Because of the slowed metabolic state, a patient can appear to be clinically dead, but there is a possibility that resuscitation can be accomplished with little or no residual neurologic deficit. It is impossible to predict the outcome based on the initial patient presentation in the field setting.

The EMT-B's initial assessment of pulse and respiration on a cold patient should take as long as 30 to 45 seconds, possibly even longer. To be sure, check the pulse for 1 minute. If the patient is determined to be pulseless and apneic, CPR should be initiated. During any patient care/resuscitation situation in which hypothermia may be a factor,

Table 7-4: Critical Trauma/Trauma Arrest

Mechanism/Indicators	EMT-B Actions
Devastating Head Trauma 1. Patient presents as unconscious and unresponsive during initial assessment, then has cardiac arrest. 2. Obvious mortal head wound. Gray matter visible.	Assess and secure airway, stabilize spine, begin CPR, contact base station for decision to transport or to discontinue resuscitative efforts.
Massive Blood Loss 1. Large amount of visible blood on patient/ground 2. Unable to produce pulse with CPR, even with increased depth of compressions	Control bleeding, reassess carotid pulse. If pulse is present, request ALS or air medical transport. Consider the use of a pneumatic antishock garment (PASG) if protocol permits. Keep patient warm. Contact base station.
Airway Obstruction 1. Patient presents in an anatomically incorrect position. 2. Poor patient color 3. Unable to ventilate	Open airway and attempt to ventilate while maintaining spinal motion restrictions. If unsuccessful, reposition jaw and attempt to ventilate again. Suction and insert oropharyngeal or nasopharyngeal airway. Repeat until obstruction is cleared.
Great Vessel Disruption 1. Poor patient color/pale 2. Unable to produce pulse even with increased depth of compressions	Reassess carotid pulse, control bleeding. Request ALS if not already done. If CPR has already been initiated, contact base station for orders, possibly to discontinue resuscitative efforts.
Tension Pneumothorax 1. Anxious patient, decreased level of consciousness 2. Extreme dyspnea 3. Distended neck veins 4. Weak, thready pulse (narrowed pulse pressure) 5. Absent breath sounds on one side 6. Tracheal deviation (late sign, often associated with cardiac arrest)	Apply high-flow oxygen by nonrebreathing mask or assist ventilations with a bag-valve-mask device. Request ALS, request air medical transport, or arrange for an ALS rendezvous.
Cardiac Tamponade 1. Anxious patient, decreased level of consciousness 2. Distended neck veins 3. Weak, thready pulse 4. Narrowed difference between systolic and diastolic numbers 5. Muffled heart tones	Request ALS or air medical transport. Contact base station for orders. Consider immediate transport. Perform CPR if cardiac arrest occurs en route.

preventing further heat loss also is a major issue. As the patient's core temperature drops, the situation becomes more critical. Remove wet clothing and cover the patient with blankets, preferably warmed. Move the patient out of the cold environment and into a warm ambulance as soon as possible. If that is not possible in the short term, steps should at least be taken to shield the patient from the wind, rain, or other elements.

Make certain that ALS is en route, because cardiac monitoring is one of the keys to keeping a handle on the patient's condition. IV access also is desirable. If ALS cannot be on scene quickly, initiate transport immediately. A hospital offers far superior technology choices for active rewarming of a patient.

Use caution during any patient handling because it is easy to precipitate ventricular fibrillation in severely hypothermic patients. Even a procedure such as endotracheal intubation has been reported to cause ventricular fibrillation in situations involving hypothermia. Field resuscitations are difficult enough without the added complications resulting from hypothermia, which makes it even harder still to resuscitate the patient successfully.

Figure 7-3 Electricity can be harmful if it enters the body.

Electrical Injuries

Most of today's modern conveniences would not be possible without electricity. Although electricity has improved our quality of life, it causes harm when it enters the body (**Figure 7-3**). Depending on the characteristics of the electrical source—for example, volts, amps, resistance, as well as the duration of the contact—the effect of exposure to electricity can range from a mild tingling sensation to cardiac arrest.

Electricity damages the body by the conversion of electric energy to heat energy as it passes through body tissues. Resistance plays a large factor as well. An intact skin surface is the most important factor impeding current flow into the body. Once the skin is cut or broken, it is far less effective in its protective qualities. The same is true (only to a lesser degree) if the skin is wet.

The voltage of the electric current also is an important factor, with high and low voltage each having unique characteristics. Low voltage follows the path of least resistance in and through the body, primarily through blood vessels, nerves, and muscle. In addition, low voltage (specifically alternating house current) is much more likely to produce ventricular fibrillation, whereas contact with direct current is more likely to produce asystole. By comparison, high voltage takes the shortest distance to reach the ground.

When an electric current passes through the brain, it can precipitate respiratory arrest. A similar result can occur if the diaphragm and other respiratory muscles are paralyzed by the electric current. This condition can persist for several minutes after the patient has been removed from the electric source. The EMT-B must be alert for these conditions. If respiratory arrest goes unrecognized and untreated for more than a minute or two, the progression of hypoxia to **anoxia** will result in a full arrest situation.

Whenever you are called to care for a possible electrical injury, remember that rescuer safety is your priority. Only when that has been addressed can patient care commence.

anoxia
An absence of oxygen in the tissues.

Training Tip

Contact the local power company and ask them to provide an inservice on the problems and hazards of working around high voltage.

Because of the many variables involved with electrical injuries, rapid assessment and management by the EMT-B are essential. This is true for all patients with electrical injury but even more so for younger patients who have little or no cardiovascular disease, which makes them easier to resuscitate. No matter what the age of the patient, you and the members of your team should aggressively resuscitate all patients with problems related to electricity exposure, even those who appear dead during the initial assessment.

All the pieces of EMT-B care need to fall quickly into place when caring for patients who have been exposed to electricity. Secure the airway, determine adequacy of breathing, and provide high-flow oxygen. Initiate CPR if indicated. If the possibility of head or neck trauma is present, take precautions to restrict spinal motion. Extinguish smoldering clothes and remove them quickly, along with any watches or constricting jewelry that may worsen tissue damage. Apply an AED immediately if the patient is pulseless and apneic.

Another pivotal decision to make is to request ALS for these patients as soon as possible. The burns and fractures commonly associated with more severe electrical injuries can warrant IV fluid replacement to counter hypovolemia. Electrical injuries can produce swelling in and around the airway, which may need ALS interventions. Extensive drug therapy also may be required, depending on the damage to and the response of the heart and cardiovascular system. In all cases involving electric shock, continuous cardiac monitoring is indicated because some cardiac rhythm disturbances absent initially may reappear as time passes.

Lightning-related Injuries

Although lightning may well be one of the most impressive and magnificent natural phenomena, it also is the most deadly, killing up to 300 Americans each year (**Figure 7-4**). Almost double that amount will sustain serious injuries as a result of their exposure to lightning.

When compared to the seemingly minute amount of electricity represented by house current, it seems miraculous that a person could survive an encounter with 100 million to possibly 2 billion volts of electricity from a lightning bolt. In fact, only about one third of those hit by lightning die. The duration of exposure is only a fraction of a second, with almost all of the current "flashing" over and around the surface of the patient, which explains the high survival rate. However, the two thirds who survive will almost all have some form of long-term disability. A small amount of the current from a lightning bolt can kill a person instantly. When this happens, the lightning strike can be thought of as a single, massive defibrillation that depolarizes the heart, usually resulting in asystole. Even if this primary cardiac event does not occur, damage

Whenever you are called to care for a possible electrical injury, always remember that rescuer safety is your priority. Only when that has been addressed can patient care commence.

No matter what the age of the patient, you and the members of your team should aggressively resuscitate all patients with problems related to electricity exposure, even those who appear dead during the initial assessment.

Figure 7-4 Lightning kills up to 300 Americans each year.

to the respiratory center in the brain or the resultant paralysis of the muscles of respiration can leave the patient in respiratory arrest. As mentioned previously, if this condition is not identified and addressed immediately, it will quickly progress into full cardiac arrest.

Another unusual characteristic of lightning is that a single strike can injure or kill multiple individuals through what often is referred to as a **splash effect**. When this occurs and multiple patients are down, a principle called **reverse triage** is employed. In this case, the dead are actually treated first, as they may be resuscitated with rescue breathing alone and cardiac arrest may be reversed.

Aside from this break from the traditional triage process, the remaining care is handled in the usual fashion. For those in respiratory arrest, rescue breathing with high concentrations of oxygen is indicated. Remember, if the respiratory arrest was precipitated by paralysis of the muscles of respiration, the patients may resume spontaneous respirations once they regain control of their musculature, allowing the rescue team to focus their resuscitative efforts on other patients.

Other therapies, such as CPR, the energy levels for defibrillation, drug sequencing, and drug dosing, all remain unchanged. Keep in mind that an unseen brain injury may have occurred, so stay alert for signs of an evolving head injury or rising intracranial pressure as indicated by changes in level of consciousness or vital signs.

Drug-related Cardiac Emergencies

Illicit drug use of both naturally occurring and synthetic substances has been documented for hundreds of years. The Aztecs were reported to be habitual users of hallucinogens, particularly psilocybin mushrooms. Cocaine use was written about in the 6th century and its use almost certainly predates that of the peoples of South America, where the coca plant is indigenous to the region.

A drug-related emergency can be thought of as either travel down the high road or the low road in terms of the body's response. Travel down the high road involves the amphetamine and amphetamine-like drugs, which include both legal (licit) as well as illegal (illicit) substances. The legal agents can be divided further into prescription and over-the-counter products (**Figure 7-5**). By comparison, travel down the low road usually is

splash effect
A situation in which a single strike of lightning injures or kills multiple individuals.

reverse triage
A method of managing a mass-casualty incident, in which the dead are treated first, as they may be resuscitated with rescue breathing alone; used in mass-casualty lightning injuries.

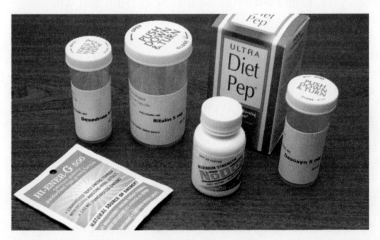

Figure 7-5 Legal substances are sold as either prescription or over-the-counter products.

brought about by heroin, other narcotics, designer analogs of narcotics, other CNS depressants, or sedative hypnotics.

The High Road

Estimates regarding cocaine use place millions of Americans as regular users. In its natural state as coca leaves, the purity is only around 2%. Once processed into cocaine hydrochloride, product purity can approach 100%. The freebase form of cocaine, or "crack" cocaine, also has high levels of purity.

The toxicity of cocaine differs for each person, and depends on the combination of purity, dose size, and method of use. For example, powdered cocaine that is sniffed may take several minutes to manifest its effects, whereas inhaling one "hit" of crack cocaine from a pipe can produce an even more intense physiologic response in less than 10 seconds.

A rapid rise in heart rate and blood pressure is common, as is chest pain, which often is what prompts a call to EMS. When cocaine is smoked, the strain on the heart, lungs, and brain is amplified, increasing the likelihood of stroke, seizure, or cardiac problems.

Possibly one of the most lethal reactions to cocaine use is decreased blood flow to the heart in combination with vasospasms that can close coronary arteries. This reaction can result in a myocardial infarction in a person who does not have blockage of a coronary artery.

For cocaine abusers with preexisting heart conditions, the body's response to cocaine can easily trigger a cardiac emergency and a call to 9-1-1. It is common for the symptoms resulting from cocaine use to resolve as the effects of the drug wear off, usually within 45 to 60 minutes. Nonetheless, the increased cardiac workload and increased oxygen consumption that accompanies it, coupled with chest pain and increased levels of anxiety and fear, may result in a call to EMS.

When confronted with a possibly drug-induced cardiac emergency, you should request an ALS response. Should the patient have a cardiac arrest, ventricular fibrillation is the most common presenting rhythm. Rapid defibrillation and excellent BLS code management are paramount to give the patient the best chance at survival. Once ALS is on scene, expect the code to follow protocol with one exception. Instead of epinephrine being given in 3- to 5-minute intervals, expect it to be administered every 5 to 10 minutes.

Designer Drugs

There are many readily available drugs, both legal and illegal, related to cocaine and amphetamines in their chemical structure as well as in their effects. Many nasal decongestants and diet aids fall into this category.

Designer drugs are compounds that have been altered in a clandestine drug laboratory setting to make them more potent and/or to skirt existing drug laws. The passage of the Designer Drug Law in the early 1980s has helped to close the legal loophole that these clandestine chemists were using, but has done little to get these drugs off the street. Methamphetamine labs are one of the most dangerous scenes any EMS provider may encounter for a variety of reasons, including toxic and flammable chemicals, carcinogenic by-products of the drug-making process, and gun-toting members of the drug trade.

Any drug that speeds up the heart also increases the heart's need for oxygen. As such, administration of high concentrations of oxygen and efforts to reduce patient anxiety are both EMT-B interventions that can be beneficial.

The Low Road

For the last few years, narcotics (specifically heroin) have been the primary drugs that have taken users down the low road to cardiac arrest. These drugs can be naturally occurring opioids such as opium and heroin, or the synthetic narcotics such as fentanyl or meperidine (Demerol). In either case, the drugs are all CNS depressants that may slow respirations to the point that the user becomes profoundly hypoxic. Again, when the heart's oxygen demands are not met, it becomes irritable, and a variety of cardiac rhythm disturbances appear. When slow heart rates result, expect the blood pressure to fall. Narcotics also cause vasodilation, which can further contribute to hypotension. Therefore, your careful monitoring of the blood pressure is a valuable contribution when caring for these patients.

The person who experiences cardiac arrest as a result of narcotic abuse may do so secondary to respiratory depression and/or respiratory arrest. Once again, the prevention of prehospital cardiac arrest is paramount. You or another EMT-B should provide assisted ventilations for patients who are breathing at fewer than 10 breaths/min or are mentating poorly. High concentrations of oxygen also are needed. If respiratory arrest occurs, effective care by you and your team may prevent cardiac arrest.

ALS providers carry with them the narcotic antagonist naloxone (Narcan). In most cases, a single dose can instantly reverse the effects of the narcotic. This may not always be the case with some of the designer narcotics, such as 3-methyl fentanyl, which is between 3,000 and 5,000 times as potent as heroin.

Tricyclic Antidepressants

tricyclic antidepressant (TCA)
A class of drug designed to treat depression; when taken in overdose concentrations, these drugs become cardiotoxic.

cardiotoxic
Describes any substance that is harmful or toxic to the heart.

In the continuing battle to fight depression, **tricyclic antidepressants (TCAs)** remain front-line drugs. When taken in the prescribed dose, it is unusual for TCAs to produce serious side effects, and to their credit, they have helped countless people live normal lives. However, when taken in excessive quantities, either accidentally or in a suicide attempt, TCAs are some of the most **cardiotoxic** medications. When taken in conjunction with alcohol, their potential lethality rises even further.

In a potential TCA overdose situation, prompt ALS response is indicated. If that is not possible, immediate transport should be initiated, as these patients can be fine one minute and crash the next. In addition to oxygen therapy, be alert for the signs and symptoms of developing TCA toxicity, which include increasing pulse rate, seizures, decreasing level of consciousness, dilated pupils, and hypotension. If a reasonably accurate time of ingestion can be identified, it can serve as a measurement tool, because most of the signs and symptoms usually are seen within $1^1/_2$ to 2 hours. As the time since ingestion moves closer to the 6-hour mark, the likelihood of toxicity decreases significantly.

The aforementioned timeframes may be helpful, but only if they are accurate. When alcohol is involved with the TCA ingestion, which it often is, any patient-reported timeframes should be considered questionable. It probably is better practice to simply stay alert for the warning signs and symptoms of TCA toxicity and provide a good hand-off report to the ALS team or the ED staff.

Considerations with Pediatric and Neonatal Resuscitation

Although it is beyond the scope and intent of this text to detail the principles and practices associated with pediatric and neonatal resuscitation, there are still some fundamental concepts that need to be covered regarding these special and challenging patient groups.

Most important, you should be thankful that cardiac arrest rarely occurs as a primary event in infants and children. Given the lack of cardiac pathophysiology, this rarity is not surprising.

Trauma mechanisms notwithstanding, cardiac arrest in infants and children almost always is secondary to respiratory insufficiency. With infants, unless a congenital defect is present, you may be certain that cardiac crisis will follow any serious unrecognized and/or untreated respiratory condition.

More often than not, in rare cases when a field delivery occurs, prompt and thorough suctioning of the newborn's airway, maintaining proper anatomic position, and being attentive for any of the signs of respiratory distress will prevent a cardiac catastrophe.

As a child grows, new variables come into play. Drowning, toxic ingestions of plants or medications, and trauma become increasingly likely as mechanisms to produce cardiac arrest. Probably the single most important point to be made about infants and children is their body's incredible ability to compensate for illness and injury. Because of this, they tend to look good until the "bottom falls out" and then physiologically crash hard. To help avoid such a catastrophe, do not unnecessarily delay transport for ill or injured children.

Wrap Up

**Chapter 7
Challenging Resuscitation Situations**

Ready for Review

While this chapter presented by no means an all-inclusive list of challenging situations, it will help you prepare for ones you will encounter most frequently. Whether the emergency call is due to stroke, electrical shock, lightning strike, trauma, or a drug-related emergency, the same basics apply. With quality EMS and excellent teamwork, the likelihood of a positive outcome is much greater in all of these cases.

Quick Case

1) You are summoned to a residence at 3:00 pm for a woman with a sudden onset of slurred speech, a drooping to the left side of her face, and a decreased ability to move the left side of her body. The patient's husband tells you that this started at approximately 2:30 pm. The patient is conscious yet confused. Her blood pressure is 144/90 mm Hg; heart rate is 76 beats/min, and respirations are 16 breaths/min and unlabored. You suspect that this patient has had a stroke.

What are the two causes of this type of stroke? What is the main benefit of getting this patient to the hospital within 3 hours of the onset of her symptoms?

_____

_____

2) After loading the patient in case #1 into the ambulance and placing the husband in the front seat, you proceed to the hospital. En route, the patient's husband tells you that his wife has chronic atrial fibrillation.

How might this cardiac rhythm have contributed to the patient's present condition?

_____

_____

3) You are dispatched to the scene of a major motor vehicle collision. On arrival, you find that there is one patient, a 24-year-old woman, who was ejected from her car after striking a tree at a high rate of speed. She is lying in a large pool of blood. You assess her and find that she is pulseless and apneic. You advise the police officer on scene to request ALS support. You begin ventilations as your partner starts chest compressions. As you assess the effectiveness of your partner's compressions, you are unable to palpate a carotid pulse.

What would explain this? Would defibrillation be successful on this patient if she were in ventricular fibrillation?

_____

_____

4 After having been submerged in icy water for approximately 20 minutes, a young man is found to have no pulse or spontaneous respirations. An ALS ambulance is not available, and the closest hospital is 30 minutes away, so you initiate immediate transport and perform CPR en route. With the patient still showing no signs of life, you contact medical control and are ordered to continue CPR.

Why continue resuscitative efforts on this patient who has been in cardiac arrest for approximately 30 minutes?

_____

_____

5 After sticking a safety pin in an electrical socket, a small child was electrocuted. When you arrive, you find that the patient is unconscious with a pulse, but is not breathing.

By which mechanism did the electrical shock stop this child's breathing?

_____

_____

6 You are dispatched to an apartment complex, where the police have just broken up a large party and discovered a young woman complaining of severe chest pain. She admits to "snorting" cocaine that night. You transport her to the hospital, where she is diagnosed with an acute myocardial infarction.

In the absence of heart disease in this patient, what is the pathophysiology behind her heart attack?

_____

_____

_____

Chapter 8

Legal Considerations

This chapter addresses a number of key legal aspects of emergency medical care. You will be warned about the potential threat of lawsuits relating to your treatment of cardiac patients or other patients who died or had another bad result, and how to protect yourself. You will learn about verbal or implied consent to treat, the extent of Good Samaritan laws, and advance directives or do not resuscitate orders. Giving depositions and other aspects of lawsuits are discussed.

Unfortunately, bad patient outcomes are part of the practice of medicine. At times, despite your attempt to deliver the best patient care, your patient will "crash." When this happens, patient care interventions increase in intensity, with the goal being to avoid a catastrophic outcome, such as death.

Although many cardiac patients are quite ill, they are not necessarily experiencing a critical life threat. Prompt prehospital interventions, provided within the standard of care, will frequently allow a safe, uneventful transport of the patient to a hospital where more definitive management of their conditions can be provided.

When a patient has a cardiac arrest in the field setting, we are no longer trying to prevent death; we are trying to reverse a death that has already occurred. The primary goal at that point should be evident: Resuscitate the patient cleanly with no neurologic deficit. As challenging as that sounds, the actual management of a patient in cardiac arrest is a routine, algorithm-driven activity. However, although the body of medical knowledge regarding the provision of emergency cardiac care continues to grow, it still is impossible to predict with certainty who will respond to care and survive a sudden death experience and who will not.

For some patients, there will be no warning whatsoever—no signs or symptoms to indicate what will come. There will be no chest pain, no progressive dyspnea, and no dull ache in the chest. They will experience sudden cardiac death.

Most patients will move through the predictable and more classic progression of signs and symptoms associated with cardiovascular disease. They will have successive cardiac-related events, increasing in frequency of occurrence as well as in severity. At some point in time, the heart will cross the pathophysiologic line of what it can tolerate. The patient will collapse, and the call to 9-1-1 will be made (**Figure 8-1**).

With the varied range of possible patient outcomes comes an equally wide range of legal and moral quandaries. Although as providers we would prefer that patient care not be complicated by legal or moral issues, it is. We need to be able to understand these issues and know how to act within the legal parameters established by federal laws or the statutes of our states and towns.

In recent years, courts have shown a tendency to support the rights of competent, informed patients to make decisions regarding whether or not to have care provided. Additionally, should they choose to be treated, the extent of the treatment and care they will receive needs to be considered. In some cases, the wishes of the patient are in direct disagreement with the position taken by the physician in charge of the patient's care (**Figure 8-2**). Such a situation is best resolved between the physician and patient to avoid involving yourself in a potential legal problem later on.

Figure 8-1 Most people with cardiovascular disease usually progress through successive cardiac-related events, eventually reaching a point that results in a call to 9-1-1.

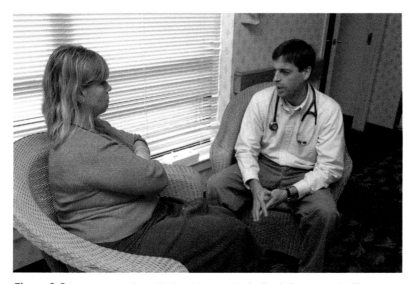

Figure 8-2 In some cases, the patient's wishes may be in direct disagreement with the physician's position.

> **M**ore than nine of 10 patients with an out-of-hospital cardiac arrest will not survive. Those who do survive rarely return to a life in which they are neurologically and physically intact.

This quandary of "what to do or what not to do" is further complicated by the reality of the current cardiac arrest survival statistics. More than nine of 10 patients with an out-of-hospital cardiac arrest will not survive. Those who do rarely return to a life in which they are neurologically and physically intact. Many of the survivors will survive for only a few days or weeks. Often, they will remain in a vegetative state until they die. Despite these undesirable outcomes, we must try to save each patient while recognizing that our attempts may fail.

Obtaining Consent to Treat

From a legal and ethical perspective, patients have the right to make decisions regarding the medical care provided to them. Although a patient might not make the same decision you or I would make, that person is still entitled to make his or her own decision. In some cases, it may be a "bad" decision, but the courts have long ago recognized that patient autonomy simply gives the right to make the decision, irrespective of whether it is good or bad. Whenever possible, medical care should be provided only after the patient has given consent. **Informed consent** is the most desirable mode in which decision making should occur. "Informed" means that the patient has a good grasp of the current medical situation and the treatment options. "Consent" represents the giving of permission as to which, if any, medical interventions will be performed. Thus, informed consent means that the patient understands the risks and benefits of the proposed plan of care as it relates to his or her particular situation, as well as the consequences that may result based on whatever choices are made by the patient.

informed consent
Permission given by a competent patient for treatment after the potential risks, benefits, and alternatives to treatment have been explained.

Implied consent is a legal premise that comes into play when a patient is in an immediate life-threatening situation but for whatever reason is unable to state his or her wishes about the provision of emergency medical care. To ensure that appropriate care is not denied because of the patient's inability to communicate, the law relative to these situations works under the assumption that the patient most likely would wish to have the life threat addressed and go on living. That implication is the basis from which the concept of implied consent has evolved.

implied consent
Type of consent in which a patient who is unable to give consent is given treatment under the legal assumption that he or she would want treatment.

Good Samaritan Laws

Good Samaritan laws and statutes exist nationwide and have gotten their name from the New Testament biblical parable. In that story, a person stopped to care for another person who was ill. From a societal perspective, the two groups of people represented were not friendly to each other and did not regularly fraternize. Even though the two groups were not friendly to each other, the Samaritan provided care.

In keeping with the spirit of the parable, Good Samaritan laws and statutes were passed to provide limited liability protection to people who, in good faith, stop to render care to an ill or injured person even though they had no legal "duty to act." These laws were focused at members of the lay public who may have little or no medical background as well as retired or "off-duty" medical professionals.

Good Samaritan laws
Statutory provisions enacted by many states to protect citizens from liability for errors and omissions in giving good faith emergency medical care, unless there is wanton, gross, or willful negligence.

Laypersons or off-duty medical professionals have no duty to act. It is not their job, at least not at the moment when they come upon a person having a medical emergency. In order to receive the protection from liability that Good Samaritan laws and statutes provide, the person providing emergency care must have no duty to act and must receive no compensation for rendering care or providing transportation to the hospital. In regard to the quality of care rendered, many of these Good Samaritan laws and statutes use what is commonly referred to as the prudent man or reasonable man doctrine, that being what a reasonable and prudent individual would have done for the patient if confronted with a similar situation. Good Samaritan laws and statutes, however, usually do not protect an individual from acts of gross negligence.

> Given the research already in existence regarding early defibrillation, many believe that shortening the time from cardiac arrest to defibrillation could be the most important advance in emergency cardiac care.

Public Access Defibrillation Legislation

One of the fastest growing areas in emergency cardiac care is in the legislative efforts regarding public access to defibrillators. Many states have either passed or are in the process of passing legislation intended to do what Good Samaritan laws and statutes are intended to do, but in this case they are focused on defibrillation using automated external defibrillators (AEDs) (**Figure 8-3**). In some cases, language about AEDs has been added to the existing Good Samaritan law/statute. As the availability of these technological wonders increases, there are hopes that the legal protection these new AED/Good Samaritan laws and statutes will provide will encourage those in close proximity to the AED to provide care to the patient with sudden cardiac arrest.

Given the research already in existence regarding early defibrillation, many believe that shortening the time from cardiac arrest to defibrillation could be the most important advance in emergency cardiac care. This belief, coupled with the reliability, ease of operation, and low maintenance of AEDs, points toward a promising future in regard to reducing mortality and morbidity for patients with sudden cardiac arrest.

Many believe that in time, AEDs will become as common and readily available as fire extinguishers, especially in places where large groups of people congregate, such as malls, offices, schools, stadiums, and theaters. Widespread deployment of AEDs also may be of particular benefit to the BLS agencies serving those living in rural America, many of whom are 20 minutes or more away from ALS providers. In that particular setting, survival rates for out-of-hospital arrest are almost zero when defibrillation is unavailable.

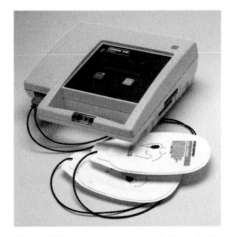

Figure 8-3 Automated external defibrillator (AED).

> In time, AEDs may become as common and readily available as fire extinguishers, especially in places where large groups of people congregate, such as malls, offices, schools, stadiums, and theaters.

Advance Directives

When they first appeared, **advance directives** (**Figure 8-4**) usually were drafted and signed with no input from the patient! Too often, patients were already mentally incapacitated and unable to make decisions about their care. Surrogate decision-makers, acting with a legal document called a durable power of attorney, made patient care and resuscitation decisions based on what they believed the patients would have wanted had they been capable of making the decision for themselves.

advance directive
Written documentation that specifies medical treatment for a competent patient should the patient become unable to make decisions; also called a living will.

With the passing of time, the concept of advance directives has expanded, in some cases going so far as to legally support the decision or wishes voiced in *conversations* between the patient and family members, the physician, and sometimes even friends. The laws and statutes relative to advance directives and **do not resuscitate orders ("DNRs")** vary from state to state and go by a variety of names and titles.

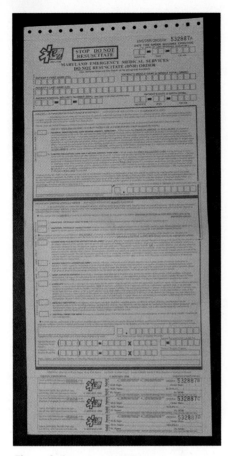

Figure 8-4 Advance directive.

do not resuscitate orders (DNRs)
Written documentation giving permission to medical personnel not to attempt resuscitation in the event of cardiac arrest.

> ### Training Tip
>
> Have an in-service for your squad on the various aspects of living wills, advance directives, DNRs, and durable powers of attorney as they apply in your state. You might want to include a lawyer or a hospital administrator in your discussions.

Without question, written directives containing the specific wishes and desires of the patient, prepared when the patient is still mentally competent, remain the most desirable and most binding in the eyes of the court system.

Unfortunately, far too often EMS responds to an emergency scene of a cardiac arrest only to be told that an advance directive specific to a DNR has been signed. If this is true, the EMS provider may think "Why was EMS called if the patient did not wish to be resuscitated?" Regardless, once on scene, the EMS team has a duty to act and care for the patient, unless legally relieved of that duty. A signed and valid advance directive with DNR instructions would serve to accomplish that. However, unless an actual printed DNR document is present, the EMS team must provide care. Even if a family member or close friend says that such a document exists, the EMS team must have physical evidence in the form of the document itself. Verbal assurances of its existence from the family will not stand up in court. Whoever is making the claim that such a document exists has the burden of proof, meaning that person must produce the document.

In a cardiac arrest situation, each minute that passes without a pulse or respirations increases the likelihood that the person cannot be resuscitated without significant neurologic deficit, if the person can be resuscitated at all. Members of the EMS team do not have the time to delay patient care in order to search for an alleged advance directive. The time spent doing so would compromise patient care, guaranteeing a poor outcome and probable death (nonresuscitation) of the patient. And, if no document is found or produced in a timely fashion, EMS would be negligent in the provision of care, or lack thereof. Therefore, if a valid advance directive can't be produced on the spot, initiate patient care activities. If the advance directive or DNR is located, a member of your team can contact medical control, relate what has transpired prior to the arrival of the document, and medical control can order that resuscitative efforts be terminated. In the case that a document is produced but is unsigned, altered, or appears suspicious for any reason, it is better to err on the side of the patient and provide care. When in doubt, run the code.

> **U**nless a valid, signed DNR document is present at the emergency scene, the EMS team must provide care.

Lawsuits

Without question, it is much better and cheaper to avoid a lawsuit than it is to have to appear in court. Still, it is important for you to know that at some point during your career, you may be involved in a lawsuit. You may be called as a witness, or you may be part of the team being sued. From a prevention standpoint, having a good bedside manner and people skills, including good communication skills, goes a long way in decreasing the probability of legal action. "Please," "Thank you," "May I," and "I'm sorry" may be some of the most important words that any prehospital provider learns to use. When providers are rude and abrasive, they indirectly communicate a lack of concern to the patient and imply to others a lack of interest in providing quality patient care.

An indication that legal action may ensue may be when you are handed a subpoena for a deposition. Depositions are not pleasant but should not be seen as the end of the world or your career. Depositions are taken in countless cases that never go to trial. To allay some of the fear associated with being deposed, you need to understand that there are three main reasons depositions are taken during the discovery phase of a lawsuit (Table 8-1).

Having excellent documentation serves a dual purpose. It is one of the best ways to avoid legal hassles as well as to defend yourself should legal action take place. Many medical malpractice cases fall under the heading of what are termed "records cases," which means there is some documentary evidence that a breach of duty exists and substandard care was the result. This breach of duty can be documentation of a wrongful action having occurred or there can be evidence of an act of omission.

The three most important things you can do to avoid a lawsuit are to provide quality patient care as specified by your service protocols and standing orders, be courteous and polite to your patient, and be sure that your patient care documentation is accurate and complete. In the unfortunate situation in which you are named in a lawsuit, these things will work in your defense and reduce the likelihood that the plaintiff will win.

Members of the EMS team do not have time to delay patient care in order to search the premises for an alleged advance directive.

If an advance directive is produced but is unsigned, altered, or appears suspicious for any reason, it is better to err on the side of the patient and provide care. When in doubt, run the code.

Table 8-1: Reasons for Depositions

- To discover the facts pertinent to the case
- To put the statements and positions of the witness on record so they can be held accountable for them later if the case goes to trial
- To evaluate the credibility of each witness

Wrap Up

Chapter 8
Legal Considerations

Ready for Review

In this chapter, you have learned about ways to protect yourself from lawsuits. You know the terms informed consent and implied consent. You understand the protection provided to you by Good Samaritan laws and that you must have a hard copy of any advance directives or DNR orders in hand, or an order from your senior medical control, to discontinue resuscitation efforts.

Quick Case

1. You are assessing a man with a history of asthma who is very anxious. He has a prescribed inhaler and has taken two puffs without relief. You explain to him that his condition warrants transport to the hospital by ambulance. You further advise the patient that oxygen therapy and another puff from his inhaler are indicated. The patient accepts your suggested treatment and recommendation for transport to the hospital.

   Of what type of consent is this an example? How does this differ from implied consent?

   _____

   _____

2. While on your way home after a busy shift, you encounter a two-car motor vehicle collision in which one of the patients is complaining of severe neck pain and is still in the vehicle. After a brief assessment, you ask that patient to step out of the car and sit on the sidewalk until EMS arrives. The patient is later diagnosed with a cervical spine fracture.

   Having provided care to this patient while off duty, are you covered by the Good Samaritan act in this particular case? Why or why not?

   _____

   _____

3. You arrive at the home of an older woman who is found to be in cardiac arrest. As you are attaching the AED, the patient's husband tells you that his wife has a living will; however, he does not know its location. He demands that you take no resuscitative action on his wife.

   Because the husband has stated that a living will exists, should you attempt resuscitation on this particular patient? Would there be any legal ramifications if you were to honor the husband's wishes?

   _____

   _____

   _____

Provider Care . . .
Taking Care of You!

*T*his chapter explores the high stress and attrition rates among EMS providers and gives you information on how to recognize when stress is affecting you or members of the EMS team. There are useful lists of the signs of short- and long-term stress responses, so you can know when you or a member of your team may need the support or help of a medical professional. Just as no chest pain should be ignored in one of your patients, the signs of stress need to be recognized and acted upon to save the job or even the life of a team member—or yourself.

In the short time that EMS has been in existence, great strides have been made in improving patient care. In retrospect, however, it seems that the tremendous progress made might have come at a high price. Almost all our efforts have focused on improving the training, education, and field performance of our field providers. Unfortunately, we have paid little attention to the well-being of caregivers.

Provider attrition has been and remains a serious problem throughout the profession (**Figure 9-1**). Although

Figure 9-1 Provider attrition remains a serious problem throughout the EMS profession.

> In recent years, EMS has finally begun to focus on addressing the well-being of the provider.

the problem tends to be much larger for those who provide care through a volunteer service provider, full-time career EMS providers are not immune to the problem. Other than a few general surveys, there is a limited body of research available.

In spite of this disturbing lack of research, we are still becoming more knowledgeable about this critical aspect of prehospital medicine. In recent years, the well-being of the provider has finally begun to be addressed. Although these efforts have certainly been a long time coming, at least we can be thankful that they are here. In truth, all the technology, techniques, and therapeutic interventions mean little without healthy, well-adjusted care providers.

Prehospital medicine frequently is provided in dynamic and often unstable settings. Potential hazards and threats to the safety and well-being of caregivers are common. Recognizing and being able to control, remove, or work around these hazards are essential skills that must be mastered. Some of the hazards that may be encountered are shown in **Figure 9-2** and include the following:

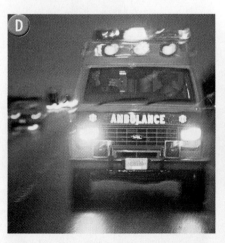

Figure 9-2 Emergencies occur anywhere and at any time. Potential threats to EMT-B safety include **A.** dangerous emergency scenes; **B.** inclement weather; **C.** hazardous materials; **D.** poorly maintained vehicles; **E.** fires or explosions; **F.** people.

- **Dangerous emergency scenes**—Emergencies can occur at any time or anywhere—highways, bar rooms, construction sites, and factories.

- **Inclement weather**—Unfavorable weather conditions may have caused or contributed to the emergency and may complicate patient care activities.

- **Hazardous materials**—Thousands of hazardous chemicals and other materials are transported and used regularly. Having a working knowledge of these materials and the additional resources that may be required to facilitate safe patient care are crucial.

- **Vehicles that are poorly maintained**—It is impossible to tell when and where the next patient may be found. Your emergency vehicle must be capable of providing safe transport for the EMS team and the patient.

- **Fire and explosion hazards**—Clandestine drug labs, especially those in the methamphetamine business, represent some of the most dangerous scenes in which to provide patient care. The precursor chemicals and the leftover waste products represent a laundry list of explosive, carcinogenic, and fire-starting or accelerant compounds. If that isn't enough, the people at the scene often are paranoid and well armed . . . a lethal situation for the unprepared provider.

- **People**—When passions run high, judgment and common sense usually run low, making people arguably the most dangerous and difficult aspect of any emergency scene.

Aside from the challenges listed above, there are additional considerations for the provider who wants to last longer than 6 months in EMS. These include the following:

- Managing stress
- Physical fitness
- Dealing with death and dying
- Poor nutritional habits
- Sleep deprivation
- Alcohol and substance abuse

Emotions, Medicine, and You

For patients and providers, unexpected illness or emergencies produce an adrenaline-fueled environment. Nowhere may those emotions run higher than when someone suddenly collapses from sudden cardiac arrest. If others are present and witness the collapse, whether they are family members, friends, or onlookers, the experience of watching someone die is overwhelming (**Figure 9-3**). When this occurs, EMS providers face one of the most daunting and challenging aspects of their job: bringing a dead patient back to life in front of family and friends. For providers and family members alike, emotions run high.

The EMT-B needs to remain calm, composed, and focused in order to provide the best care possible. The EMT-B also has to keep the family and friends at the scene informed and be attentive to them because they are in need of care as well.

Figure 9-3 The experience of watching someone die is overwhelming for everyone, including EMS providers.

Table 9-1: Warning Signs of Stress

Warning Signs—Initial Stress Response

- Increased heart and respiratory rate
- Elevated blood pressure
- Dilated pupils
- Cool, sweaty skin
- Difficulty concentrating
- Inability to make decisions
- Sleep disturbances

Warning Signs—Extended Stress Response

- Personality changes (guilt, depression)
- Chronic fatigue
- Work problems (tardiness, coworker disputes, cynicism)
- Alcohol/drug abuse
- Change in appetite
- Decreased interest in sex

When stress levels overwhelm a provider's coping capabilities and mechanisms, it is important to recognize what is happening and get the provider the help he or she needs.

The Stress of EMS

The field of prehospital medicine may well be one of the most stressful of all the branches of medicine. Typically, a sudden, unexpected medical or traumatic event occurs, interrupting the daily routine of work or home life, prompting a call to 9-1-1. When compared to the clean, controlled medical environment of a hospital, prehospital medicine unfolds anywhere, anytime, and frequently under what only can be described as adverse circumstances. High levels of stress can be everywhere.

To be an effective prehospital care provider, you must understand the common causes of stress, how to recognize the warning signs and symptoms of stress overload, and what actions to take if you see these signs or symptoms in yourself or a coworker.

Realize that stress in and of itself is not a bad thing. In the right amounts, it can push your body and mind to rise to meet the challenge and bring you to even higher levels of performance. It is when stress becomes excessive and exceeds your usual coping skills and stress management mechanisms that it can render you overwhelmed and finally ineffective as a caregiver. There are two categories of warnings that your body will give when you are experiencing stress: the initial or immediate stress response, and the extended or delayed stress response (Table 9-1).

Both forms of excessive stress need to be addressed right away, because both affect your ability to make the key decisions required of a good EMT, and both are bad for your physical and emotional health. For example, if you try to ignore the initial stress response, either your own or that of a member of your team, it may result in loss of scene control and dangerously substandard patient care. This stress-induced inability to manage a call or to provide standard patient care may, in worst-case scenarios, result in a lawsuit, death of a patient, or in the loss of public confidence in your EMS team.

Sadly, there are many emergency care providers who fail to accept that stress is a daily part of life in EMS. Long hours, poor diet, sleep deprivation, sleep pattern disruption, and uncooperative patients can combine to slowly unravel the fabric of a provider. One disastrous event, such as a mass-casualty incident or the death of a child, could leave you or one of your team members incapable of functioning normally. The suicide or accidental death of one of your team can be a life-changing event, and it may even cause you or another team member to consider leaving the profession altogether. The day-to-day stressors present in prehospital medicine can be subtle, taking their toll over a period of weeks, months, and even years. Don't be fooled into thinking that those extended time-frames don't make chronic stress less damaging. They just make it harder to identify.

When stress levels overwhelm a provider's coping capabilities and mechanisms, it is important to recognize what is happening and get the provider the help he or she needs. Increasingly, private and municipal services are setting up employee assistance programs to help care for their providers. Although the informal support network that exists among providers is invaluable (Figure 9-4), there are times when professional intervention may be required to turn around a situation in hopes of salvaging a career.

In addition to the support and corrective interventions employee assistance programs can provide, there are some simple changes that you can make or help others make right away.

- **Match expectations with reality.** If EMS providers think that they can or should save all of their patients, they are wrong. If they think that they will get 8 hours of uninterrupted sleep a night so that they are refreshed and ready to go to their part-time job, they are wrong again. When the expectations of a job don't match its reality, providers can become disgruntled, disillusioned, and disappointed quickly. Before you know it, one of the team is gone, adding to the attrition problem in EMS.

- **Take time for yourself and have a life outside of EMS.** Taking time off is essential to your well-being. Learn to say no to the endless opportunities for overtime shifts. Have friends, hobbies, and outside interests. Separate your work life from your life outside of work as much as possible. Make the commitment to a regular physical fitness or exercise program and stick with it. Try to eat healthy foods.

- **Don't waste your career complaining about things you can't change.** Realize and accept that every industry has its problems, not just EMS. Each business has people who use and abuse its privileges. Patients are not always grateful. Understand that saving lives is not a daily event and that nonemergent medicine makes up most of what EMS is all about. Recognize that life isn't always fair and that bad things happen to nice people through no fault of your own.

Figure 9-4 Informal support among providers is invaluable, but sometimes professional intervention may be required to help you or a coworker.

Teamwork and EMS

Success in the field of EMS is invariably linked to the ability of the EMS providers and other responders to blend together quickly into a cohesive team. There may be no better example of that than in the realm of emergency cardiac care and advanced cardiac life support. Think about the following scenario: A customer in the checkout line at the local grocery store collapses from sudden cardiac arrest. Local first responders are on scene in minutes and administer CPR. An EMT-B squad with defibrillation capabilities from the neighboring community is another minute or two behind. They shock the patient twice into a perfusing rhythm and continue to assist respirations as they initiate transport. A few miles out of town, they rendezvous with a paramedic unit that assumes care and continues to stabilize the patient throughout the remaining 17 minutes of transport to the hospital. At the hospital, the paramedics provide a hand-off report, and the ED staff assumes care of the patient. The ED staff sends the patient to the catheterization lab, where an occluded coronary vessel is reopened. After a brief stay in the Coronary Care Unit, your patient is discharged and goes home to his family.

In this scenario, it is essential to recognize that *no single aspect* of a call is more important than any other. Each provider who cared for the patient was essential to the patient's successful outcome.

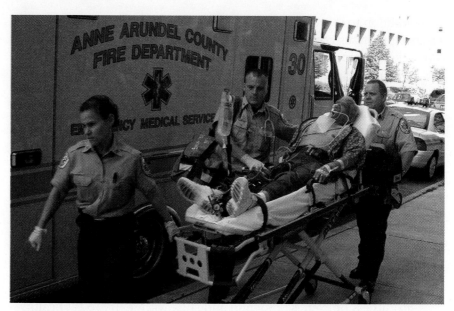

Figure 9-5 BLS and ALS teamwork improves the likelihood of a positive patient outcome.

It is your skill and successful teamwork in EMS, and specifically in emergency cardiac care, that are the focus of this text and the associated coursework that it accompanies (**Figure 9-5**). The goal is to make you a better-educated, better-trained EMT-B who can make well-informed positive contributions when working with ALS providers on cardiac patients. You are a key player in a team that increases the chance of a positive outcome for your patient.

We provide care to many thousands of patients with cardiac-related emergencies each year. This care needs to be as seamless as possible, with all providers doing their respective jobs to the best of their abilities, followed by providing accurate hand-off reports at each step. Positive, caring attitudes need to shine through from start to finish. Only one person truly suffers when the EMS system fails to perform as it should—the patient.

Again, the quality of the emergency cardiac care we deliver directly depends on each provider involved in the continuum of patient care. That's why it is important to take care of yourself so that you can provide quick, decisive care to the best of your abilities.

Death and Dying

One of the most difficult aspects of EMS and specifically emergency cardiac care is dealing with poor outcomes, such as the death of a patient. One of the most important skills any medical provider can acquire is how to cope with and come to terms with the death of a patient. This is especially difficult for those in medicine who may see patients die each day. During the initial training of providers, many programs teach and reinforce the idea that if the provider does all the right things, in the right sequence and within appropriate timeframes, there will be a positive outcome. Sadly, outside the classroom setting that is not the case. In spite of what you as the provider may learn from a patient regarding the emergency at hand, at best you probably know only a fraction of what has precipitated the cardiac crisis with which you are confronted.

It is essential for you to accept that even when all your responses and interventions are appropriate and timely, some of your patients will die because their hearts were already too damaged to respond to all the techniques, technology, and therapeutics that emergency cardiac care and advanced cardiac life support have to offer. Perhaps the facts will help you accept that death will occur. Historically, we know that most patients (about 95%) who are found in cardiac arrest at an emergency scene will be past the point of resuscitation. You are there to do the best you can with every patient, so that there is a possibility of life for the patient. Do not take a patient's death as a personal failure. Your job is to provide each patient with 100% of your skill and decision-making ability. Do your best. In cases where your best efforts don't keep the patient alive, remember that your best *is* all that you can do. Although 5% survival rates for cardiac arrest experienced out of hospital are very discouraging, keep in mind that *without* EMS interventions, that survival rate would be 0%.

Anticipated Death

From a practical perspective, there are two categories of death: anticipated and acute. Each comes with its own circumstances and challenges.

In the case of anticipated death, a family member has been diagnosed with a terminal condition, and the choice has been made for the person to die at home (**Figure 9-6**). Historically, our culture has done little, if anything, to prepare family members and loved ones. The neat, sterile, stoic death we've seen on television, where someone utters a profound statement or two then turns the head to the side and quietly slips into death, rarely, if ever, occurs. Often, a run of ventricular tachycardia or other cardiac

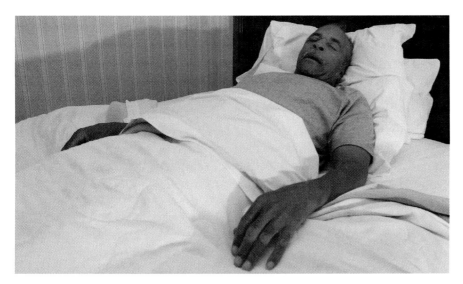

Figure 9-6 In the case of anticipated death, a family member has been diagnosed with a terminal condition, and the choice has been made for the person to die at home.

arrhythmia causes the patient's brain to become hypoxic. The patient collapses to the floor, in some cases seizes as the brain malfunctions from having inadequate oxygen available to meet its metabolic needs. Seizures can be quite violent and frightening for family members. When the patient goes into cardiac arrest, the skin assumes the bluish-gray tint of cyanosis. The plans to have a relative die a quiet, dignified death are disrupted by a much more harsh reality. In anticipated deaths, it usually is at this late stage that 9-1-1 is called. As the EMS provider arriving on the scene, you may know that it is too late or simply impossible to resuscitate the patient, but you face the task of dealing with a family frightened by the stark realities of death and unsure of what to do without a medical person in the home.

When you arrive at the scene in response to the call for assistance, you begin patient care. After you have begun efforts to resuscitate, someone in the home tells your team of the patient's terminal condition and his or her wish to die at home. A difficult situation confronts you at that point. Under the premise of implied consent, you have initiated care on an unconscious, unresponsive patient. The law does not give friends or family members the authority to stop the treatment. An appropriate question for you to ask of the family as one of your team continues attempts at resuscitation might be "What exactly would you like us to do?" If the person claims that a living will or advance directive has been signed, then they must produce a copy of a valid, signed document, as discussed in Chapter 8. If the person wants resuscitative efforts to cease, base station or physician contact is usually required.

Acute Death

While *all* life-ending events are extremely stressful, the shock of an acute unexpected event is even more so. Again, resuscitation efforts must be promptly initiated to optimize survival chances for the patient (**Figure 9-7**). At the same time, several other actions need to occur.

In this situation, as you set up to begin resuscitation efforts, have a team member remove the family to another room or area away from the resuscitation efforts. Even a well-run resuscitation is disturbing to watch. Allowing distraught family members or friends to remain present only adds to their anxiety and yours. The additional pressure of having family members watch may distract members of the EMS team from the many tasks they need to perform quickly. Some studies, however, have shown that family members benefit from watching the resuscitation effort because it helps bring closure to the situation if the effort is unsuccessful.

If the choice has been made for the family to be sequestered, one of your team members will need to keep them informed periodically as to the status of the patient and of the resuscitation. All statements you or your team members make to the family should be made with compassion and be clear and informative. A comment such as "Well, it was going okay, but your wife kind of slipped through the cracks" only leaves family and friends confused and uncertain as to what you mean. It would be more appropriate to say "I'm sorry, we did everything we could, but your wife is dead."

In most cases, you and the other members of the EMS team will have a feel for how treatment is going based on the response or lack of response of the patient to your patient care interventions. A progression of

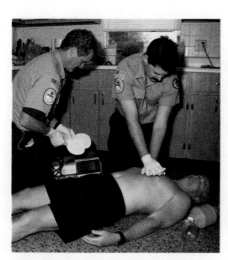

Figure 9-7 Resuscitation efforts must be promptly initiated to optimize survival chances for the patient.

statements shared with family members by one of your team at periodic intervals usually causes less stress than leaving them uninformed for 30 minutes and letting their anxiety build (**Figure 9-8**). An ongoing sharing of information in more manageable bits and pieces prepares them better for what frequently is going to happen—an unsuccessful resuscitation and the death of their loved one.

Grief and the Grieving Process

<u>Grief</u> is defined as deep sorrow or mental distress caused by loss, remorse, or affliction. As mentioned previously, coping with the death of another human being is a powerful, stressful event. Those present can react in a number of ways as the emotion of the experience starts to sink in. Unfortunately, one of the most common responses is to verbally lash out in anger at the EMS team. When this occurs, it is essential to realize that while unpleasant and challenging to deal with, anger is a normal human response. Again, it is important for you not to take the verbal and angry attack as an attack on you personally. Because you know about stress responses, grief, and other emotions relating to death, you realize that you and your team are the most convenient targets for the frustrations of those present who have just lost a friend or loved one. This knowledge may help temper your own response or may help you keep another team member from losing control.

After an initial display of grief, those involved in the death will at some point in time need to accept what has happened. To get to that point, people often move through any or all of the various stages of grieving (Table 9-2).

Recognize also that grieving is a personal matter and varies from one person to another. One person may be angry and then in a few days or so quickly come to grips with the situation and realizes that a loved one is dead. Others may be in denial, ie, "He can't be dead!" As time passes, they may then move into bargaining, ie, "If they could only be here now, things would be different." This process may take weeks, months, or even years.

Still others may never overcome the grief, and over time their unresolved grieving may well become a life threat for the survivor. Think of a couple who were married happily for 50 years and then suddenly one of them dies. Three months later, the other mate dies. It is difficult to make a compelling argument that this is a coincidence.

Your goals when communicating and dealing with family members and friends about death should be as follows:

- Be honest and direct, yet compassionate
- Be respectful of the seriousness of the situation
- Use clear, easily understandable, and descriptive language
- Treat the needs of the survivors

Reaching Out to Others

Some final thoughts on the matter of provider care include another difficult challenge and one that requires a proactive approach to truly be successful. It involves *caring for each other.*

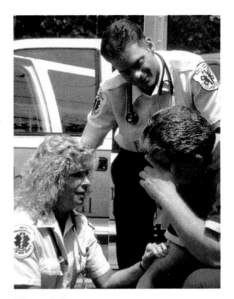

Figure 9-8 Sharing information at periodic intervals with family members or friends at the scene helps manage their stress.

<u>grief</u>
A deep sorrow or mental distress caused by loss, remorse, or affliction.

Table 9-2: The Five Stages of Grieving
• Anger
• Denial
• Depression
• Bargaining
• Acceptance

There are laws and statutes mandating patient care, but there are no laws or statutes that require that we provide care to our EMS teams. No laws require any EMS providers to stop what they are doing, turn around, and ask their partner any of the following questions:

- Why did you yell at and berate the last patient?
- Why have you smelled of alcohol at the start of the last two shifts?
- Why have you recently started sitting alone between calls?

That sample list represents no more than the tip of an emotional iceberg. Countless more examples could and should be added if we as EMS professionals are committed to caring not only for our patients but for each other as well. We are in a profession where at a moment's notice, multiple providers from multiple agencies or disciplines are asked to work together on behalf of one or more patients. It is easier to walk away from a coworker's problems than to walk back and offer your help and support. A holistic approach to caring for caregivers is needed if we are committed to the well-being of those who spend their time in the trenches of prehospital medicine.

Wrap Up

Chapter 9
Provider Care ... Taking Care of You!

Ready for Review

In this chapter, you have learned all about the high stress and attrition rates among EMS providers and how to recognize signs of short- and long-term stress responses. Our communication with and care for others in our own profession deserves the same clarity, attention, and compassion that we give to patients and their families. By taking better care of ourselves and helping others on our team to learn and practice positive self-care, we are improving our lives and our ability to help our patients.

Quick Case

1. You are a brand new EMT-B and are working your first shift. A call comes in for a 6-month-old child in full cardiac arrest. Despite you and your partner's best efforts, you are unsuccessful in resuscitating the child. When you return to the station, you tell your partner that you don't think you will be able to handle this line of work.

   What lifestyle adjustments must you make if you are to remain effective in the field of EMS? You feel that your heart rate is "beating a mile a minute." What is causing this uncomfortable feeling?

   _____

   _____

2. At the start of a shift, you receive a call for a patient with a minor injury. Your partner, an EMS veteran of 17 years, tells the patient in a rude tone of voice that he should not have called EMS for a minor injury. The patient, however, wishes to be transported to the hospital. When you complete the call and arrive back at the station, your partner lashes out at you for no apparent reason. As he is shouting in your face, you note the possible smell of alcohol on his breath.

   How can you best help your partner? What would happen if you were to ignore his behavior?

   _____

   _____

   _____

Chapter 10

Putting It All Together

T hus far you have learned about the components of ACLS. This chapter helps put it all together into the context of what you could do during one emergency ACLS call.

In advanced cardiac life support, people, technical expertise, protocols, selected technology, and therapeutic interventions must be combined quickly and efficiently into a seamless cohesive effort. When all these parts are put together, the intent is the reduction of patient mortality and morbidity.

Listed below are the nine key ingredients needed to provide optimal ACLS care.

1. Early Access to ALS

It is becoming increasingly common for BLS services to make arrangements with ALS services to respond either directly to the scene or to provide an ALS rendezvous. Both approaches focus on the same goal: delivering the same quality of prehospital care that people experience in the urban setting not only to the suburbs, but even further into the rural parts of our country.

When ALS responds to the emergency scene in coordination with a BLS crew, it is termed a tiered or layered response. Your BLS team arrives first and does the initial patient assessment and work-up. On the basis of criteria predefined by local protocol, you then decide whether to request an ALS response. Your task is to perform the initial tier of emergency medicine: identify and correct life threats, call for ALS, keep the patient alive, and begin to stabilize the patient. Without this tier, there is no second tier. The second tier is the ALS team, which brings additional therapies to stabilize the patient further.

With an ALS rendezvous, your BLS crew also assesses and does the initial work-up on the patient. You or the dispatcher sets up the place where the ALS team will meet you. Your team provides the appropriate care interventions as you load the patient and initiate transport. The ALS unit goes to a preselected rendezvous site. When your BLS unit arrives, at least one and possibly two ALS providers join your BLS unit with their gear, and transport continues. The ALS team performs an assessment and provides ALS care en route to the hospital.

In either case, the real key to providing quality care is to be proactive in requesting ALS support. Your task as the first tier provider is to make a prompt, informed, and insightful patient assessment, and then make the call for ALS support.

Savvy BLS service providers usually adapt some of the decision making used in criteria-based emergency dispatching outlined by local protocol in deciding whether to request ALS. That, coupled with a solid initial assessment, gets ALS en route sooner, hopefully before the one-and-two-and-three-and-four activity gets started. Ideally, ALS and BLS combine their respective efforts and *prevent the prehospital cardiac arrest from occurring*. Just remember, by making a timely call to your ALS provider, you will have ALS support sooner, and early access to ALS care means a better outcome for your patient. ALS care is built on BLS care (**Figure 10-1**). ALS interventions are too often ineffective if BLS interventions were not provided first or were not done effectively.

2. Cardiopulmonary Resuscitation

One of the most important contributions EMT-Bs can make in emergency cardiac care and specifically in cardiac arrest management is to provide the most effective CPR as possible.

Figure 10-1 ALS care is built on BLS care.

It has been said that effective CPR produces at best a third of the cardiac output and perfusion that the body does. A third of normal output is not much. What is scarier to consider is that with ineffective CPR, the output is lower than one third.

Ideally, each compression should produce a palpable pulse, and the patient should begin to pink up or, in people with dark pigmented skin, become less cyanotic. Ventilations should be timely, in the right sequence, and of adequate depth to provide good oxygenation with the subsequent lowering of carbon dioxide (CO_2) levels, followed by intubation and the securing of a patent airway occurring as soon as possible.

The relationship of CO_2 levels and the body's pH is very important in emergency medicine. As CO_2 levels rise, the body's pH falls, and the patient becomes increasingly acidotic (**Figure 10-2**). Coupled with the already poor metabolism that occurs during CPR and the many acidic waste products ineffective metabolism produces, the patient's slide into acidity is rapid. Keep in mind that normal pH is 7.35 to 7.45, and that 6.9 is the lowest level of pH considered compatible with life. Effective CPR can help slow that potentially fatal slide into acidity.

Another key feature of CPR is that it provides the mechanism whereby the various cardiac drugs are delivered to the heart and the body. These drugs are ineffective if they are puddled in an arm just above the IV site instead of being pumped to the heart.

Finally, you can be especially helpful by knowing when to start and stop CPR without having to be reminded. Prior to a defibrillation attempt, CPR stops and everyone clears the patient. If the shock is ineffective and CPR is indicated again, it needs to occur promptly. If you are one of the EMT-Bs performing CPR, make sure you know when to stop and when to resume CPR.

3. Airway Control and Oxygen Therapy

Airway control and administration of oxygen are other areas in which you can assist the ACLS team. Airway control and provision of effective

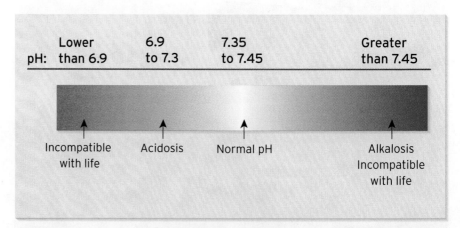

Figure 10-2 As CO_2 levels rise, the body's pH falls, and the patient becomes increasingly acidotic. Effective CPR can help slow the potentially fatal slide into acidity.

respiratory support in the form of oxygen therapy are cornerstones of good care for all patients, but especially cardiac patients.

Oxygen

By providing supplemental oxygen to the patient as quickly as possible and in high concentrations, you may prevent just a little less myocardium from dying, or you may even prevent the patient from going into cardiac arrest, therefore increasing the patient's chances of a good outcome.

Suction

It is important to have the suction unit ready. You know that nausea frequently accompanies heart attacks and that if patients vomit, their airway may become blocked and require suction.

Intubation

EMT-Bs who do not perform intubation can help facilitate a quick intubation by performing any or all of the following functions to assist those who do (**Figure 10-3**):

- Preoxygenation of the patient
- Equipment selection and check
- Suction — is it ready to go?
- Perform the **Sellick maneuver** (**Figure 10-4**)

Once the intubation is performed, tube placement confirmed, and the tube has been secured in place, there is still key airway control work that you can do.

- Monitor and periodically reassess breath sounds
- Ventilate the patient via the ET tube with a BVM device with oxygen reservoir
- Monitor tube position for slippage/displacement

EMT-Bs who can be counted on to either perform or assist with these activities will free up the paramedic(s) to do other tasks that they alone must perform.

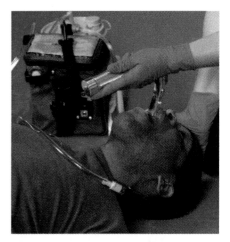
Figure 10-3 EMT-Bs can help facilitate quick intubation.

Sellick maneuver
A technique used with intubation, in which pressure is applied on either side of the cricoid cartilage to prevent gastric distention and allow better visualization of vocal cords; also called cricoid pressure.

> ## Training Tip
>
> Have an inservice with your ALS provider and learn the layout of the airway kit. Better yet, track down an intubation manikin and practice intubation.

4. Cardiac Monitoring

About 90% of the cardiac patients who die of lethal heart rhythms do so within the first hour after their heart attack. Therefore, you will need to stay alert for the signs of impending disaster. One of the classic red flags is when the ventricles become irritable and begin to attempt to pace the heart. The beats that come from the ventricles early in the cardiac cycle

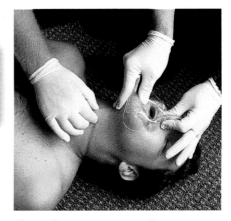
Figure 10-4 Performing the Sellick maneuver can facilitate intubation. Apply firm pressure on the cricoid ring with your thumb and index finger on either side of the midline. Maintain pressure until the patient is intubated.

premature ventricular contractions (PVCs)
Contractions of the heart's ventricles that come earlier than normal, often leading to ventricular tachycardia or ventricular fibrillation.

are called **premature ventricular contractions (PVCs)**. These warning PVCs often indicate a slide into ventricular tachycardia or ventricular fibrillation. If you are familiar enough with your heart rhythms and can see these PVCs on the screen, immediate treatment can prevent this slide from happening. With so many other patient care activities occurring, it is easy to miss a couple of PVCs here and there as they fly across the ECG screen. If you know what they are and what they look like, you will have a better chance of catching them. Bring this to the attention of an ALS team member who can respond with treatment.

False Signals

Be alert for sources of 60-cycle electrical interference, which include electric blankets and microwave ovens. If you can recognize 60-cycle electrical interference on the screen and eliminate the source of the interference, you can instruct someone to locate the source and turn it off, keeping the monitor doing its proper task of monitoring the patient's electrical impulses. You may also have artifact from poor contact with an electrode. The solution is to press the electrode down firmly to make solid contact with the patient's chest or replace it, if necessary. Eliminating the artifact will help to provide a more clear, readable tracing.

This course is not intended to give you the capabilities to read the more than 50 cardiac rhythms most ALS providers can identify, but it gives the fundamentals of the basic sinus rhythms as well as some background on the most lethal rhythms that you are likely to encounter.

Don't forget to do pulse checks after *any* rhythm changes on the monitor (**Figure 10-5**). The cardiac monitor only identifies whatever electrical activity is present. It does not in any way guarantee that what you are seeing is producing a pulse for your patient. That is up to you to determine!

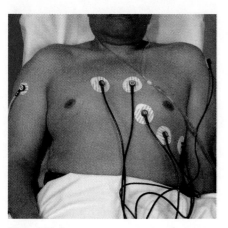

Figure 10-5 It is important to do pulse checks after any rhythm changes on the monitor.

Training Tip

Learn how and where to apply electrodes for at least lead II and ideally for any lead configuration your ALS provider normally uses.

5. Intravenous Therapy

Starting an intravenous (IV) lifeline on a scared, sweaty cardiac patient is not easy. It is a fine-motor skill that any good field medic will continue to polish throughout his or her career. A big part of that skill is making a wise choice of vein selection. Under ideal circumstances, finding the right vein takes a moment or two, and on a very sick cardiac patient it may take even longer.

You can help by using this time to find the right bag of IV fluid, hook up the administration set, and flush the tubing so that everything is all set and ready to go when the medic finds the vein to be cannulated.

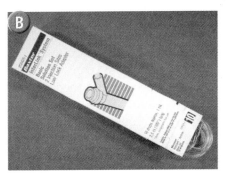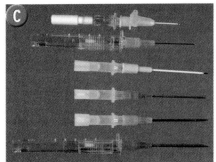

Figure 10-6 Some equipment used to start an IV. **A.** IV fluid bags. **B.** Administration set. **C.** Catheters.

The following is a list of IV equipment with which you should become familiar (**Figure 10-6**):

- Constricting band
- Alcohol/povidone iodine preparation
- IV fluid
- Administration set
- IV catheters (2)
- Tape
- 4 × 4s or 2 × 2s
- Op site

Once the IV has been started, you can help by picking up any sharps and disposing of them in the sharps container (**Figure 10-7**). This step is an important safety and body substance isolation service. No one needs the stress of an accidental needle stick as a result of careless sharps handling.

During the course of the call, you will want to watch the IV bag and chamber to be certain that fluid continues to drip regularly into the drip chamber on the IV tubing, which will help to confirm that the IV is still patent and running. If you see it stop dripping and/or you notice swelling at the IV site, this may indicate that the IV has blown and is no longer functioning. You can alert the paramedic immediately so he or she can restart the IV. In some cases, drugs that infiltrate into body tissue can be harmful, so let the paramedic know as soon as you notice that the IV is not working properly.

Figure 10-7 Once an IV has been started, pick up any sharps and dispose of them in the sharps container.

Training Tip

Learn where the various IV solutions are kept in the ALS rig and in the jump kits. Have an inservice on how to properly set them up.

6. Drug Therapy

Without your BLS interventions, the patient may die, but BLS alone may not be enough to keep the patient from dying. Really sick patients often need the benefits that the ALS team and pharmacology have to offer. Giving the right amount of the appropriate drug within the specified time takes a concentrated effort by the paramedic. In addition, paramedics always must consider the possible interactions that occur when cardiac drugs given in the field react with any drugs the patient may already be taking.

Your contributions in the drug administration process are to find and hand over quickly any medication the paramedic requests. You might think it makes more sense for the paramedic to keep the drug box close enough to simply reach in and take the drug he or she needs for the patient. Sometimes that is the case. However, the experienced paramedic realizes that an alert and oriented but frightened patient may become more alarmed when he sees the drug box open with its multiple drawers of medications. Imagine you are going to the dentist, already nervous. You walk in and see a tray set up with 40 different kinds of probes, pokers, and scrapers. Just seeing that massive display of sharp stainless steel would probably make you even more nervous. Compare your imagined fear at the dentist to the magnitude of fear that the heart patient is feeling, thinking that he or she may die. Keeping the medication box out of the patient's sight helps keep the patient from becoming even more frightened.

7. Defibrillation

Rapid defibrillation relies on the prompt recognition of ventricular fibrillation. An extra set of eyes on the monitor increases the likelihood that it will be picked up as soon as it happens. Those eyes could be yours.

In many systems, defibrillation is a skill that you may perform as an EMT-B. Make certain that you have practiced this skill until it is second nature, because this skill often is performed in one of the most stressful environments with distraught family members, friends, or bystanders looking on.

Remember that the person who is going to push the button to fire the defibrillator is ultimately responsible for the safe operation of the defibrillator. The three components of safe defibrillation, discussed in Chapter 5, are once again listed in **Table 10-1**. Team members may be so focused on performing a skill that they do not hear the command to stand back. It is critical to clear the team verbally and visually before defibrillation.

In the event of a rhythm change from the shocked rhythm to what should now be a perfusing rhythm, make certain that there is a pulse check. Again, it is essential to remember that the cardiac monitor only displays electrical activity within the heart. It does not guarantee a perfusing rhythm.

Table 10-1: Steps to Safe Defibrillation

1. Confirm that the patient is pulseless, apneic, in cardiac arrest, and in VF or pulseless VT.

2. Make absolutely certain that you are clear of any patient contact.

3. Confirm that other members of the rescue team are clear of any patient contact.

8. Documentation

As mentioned previously, one of the biggest differences between treatment in the field and treatment in the hospital is access to resources. Trying to accomplish all that needs to be done with two or three people in the field is far different than with eight or nine.

While being the person in charge of the flow chart at a cardiac arrest doesn't sound like an exciting job, it is essential. If you are the person holding the chart, and you have accurate times as to when the various drugs were administered, procedures were performed, or defibrillations were delivered, you help link all the activities together. If the patient starts to deteriorate or doesn't progress as quickly or in the direction that is expected, the flow chart can serve as a quick and handy reference to review. For example, if epinephrine is supposed to be given every 3 to 5 minutes throughout the time that the resuscitation goes on, while you are writing you can also glance at your watch and let the medic know when it's time to administer the epinephrine again. Managing the chart or run report is another way that you as an EMT-B can contribute to the provision of optimal ACLS care to your patients.

What if months or maybe even years after the call you find out that the unfortunate side effect of a lawsuit is going to unfold? An accurate run report is the single best defense tool at your disposal in case of a deposition or lawsuit.

9. Scene Choreography

You may be the most unrecognized and unsung hero of any call if you are the person who provides the choreography of the emergency scene. While the dramatic events are unfolding, there are scores of small, seemingly mundane tasks that can make the call run more smoothly and effectively. As you know, every call is different and has many variables that must be addressed as they arise. This makes it impossible to provide you with a master list of what should be done on every call. We can remind you of some things to consider as you choreograph your next call.

- **Secure any possible pesky pets.** Dogs in particular develop an affection for the hand that feeds them and will try to protect that person. While you may well think that CPR is a benign procedure, a dog may see this as an attack on its owner. It is best to secure pets in a bathroom or bedroom or anywhere they can be guaranteed to stay out of the way.

- **Shuttle equipment.** During a call, various pieces of equipment need to both come and go. This is where your logistical thinking comes in. Knowing which equipment to move out of the way and which equipment needs to stay close at hand is important. During treatment this is even more important. You can keep the scene uncluttered by getting extra equipment out of the way. Field codes (cardiac arrests) are messy enough without having additional obstacles. Also, putting things back where they came from while the ALS team is at work means you are loaded and ready to go when the time comes to initiate patient transport.

- **Isolate family members and friends.** A cardiac arrest resuscitation, even one that is being well run, can be very upsetting to onlookers. In EMS, we see them often enough that we usually don't appreciate how harsh resuscitation looks to others. Tubes going down airways, multiple IV sticks, defibrillation, and even CPR are not pleasant things to watch being done to someone you love or care about.

Gather family and friends together in a kitchen or other room so they don't have to witness the resuscitation. Equally important, don't forget that they are in there. Every few minutes, as time permits or as the situation changes, step in and give the family or friends a brief update. It may only take you a minute to do that, but the look on their faces will tell you how much they appreciate anything you have to tell them and how hard it is to wait.

- **Provide access and egress.** There needs to be a clear path both in and out of the scene for both people and equipment. Besides being able to get ALS personnel and equipment in and out, you will need to have room for a quick exit for the patient on the ambulance cot. Getting furniture out of the way by pushing it aside and clearing the floor of lamps, toys, or other small objects will keep care providers from tripping or falling, and hurting themselves or kicking out the IV line.

Being able to put all the individual pieces of the treatment plan together is essential if we are to provide quality care. There are many pieces — the patient, the BLS team and equipment, and the ALS team and equipment; each call is unique. ACLS is quite challenging. With all members of the EMS team, both ALS and BLS, working in harmony, a positive patient outcome is more likely.

Wrap Up

**Chapter 10
Putting It All Together**

Ready for Review

This chapter reviewed the nine areas in which the EMT-B can take steps to provide optimal ACLS patient care:

1. Early access to ALS
2. CPR
3. Airway control and oxygen therapy
4. Cardiac monitoring
5. IV therapy
6. Drug therapy
7. Defibrillation
8. Documentation
9. Scene choreography

By assisting in these areas during ACLS care, the EMT-B can make a significant, life-saving contribution.

Quick Case

1. While performing CPR on a patient who has been in cardiac arrest for a period of approximately 5 minutes, your partner brings in the AED, analyzes the cardiac rhythm, and delivers three shocks as indicated.

   As you resume CPR, what signs would you expect to see if your chest compressions were effective? What are your goals in providing artificial ventilations?

   _____

   _____

2. During the course of managing a patient with a suspected acute myocardial infarction, you apply a nonrebreathing mask and set the flow rate at 15 L/min in order to deliver 100% supplemental oxygen.

   What therapeutic effects does oxygen have on an evolving myocardial infarction?

   _____

   _____

3. You are assisting a paramedic in intubating an unconscious, apneic patient who has a palpable carotid pulse. The paramedic asks you to provide cricoid pressure.

   Of what benefit will this be to the paramedic? Of what benefit will it be to the patient?

   _____

   _____

4 Considering the skills that are within the EMT-B's scope of practice, how can you be most effective as a team member when assisting an ALS crew with each of the following techniques?

    a.   Endotracheal intubation

    b.   Intravenous therapy

    c.   Medication administration

    d.   Overall management of the scene

_____

_____

_____

Glossary

access port: A sealed hub on an administration set designed for sterile access to the fluid.

adenosine: A naturally occurring substance produced in the body; also used as a drug in cardiac medicine to slow conduction through the middle of the heart and restore normal sinus rhythm.

administration set: Tubing that connects to the IV bag access port and the catheter in order to deliver the IV fluid.

advance directive: Written documentation that specifies medical treatment for a competent patient should the patient become unable to make decisions; also called a living will.

advanced cardiac life support (ACLS): The provision of emergency cardiac care using invasive techniques or technology.

ALS rendezvous: A model for patient care in which the BLS team receives the call and arranges for ALS providers to meet them at an agreed-upon location, resulting in providing ACLS care to the patient as soon as possible.

alveoli: The air sacs of the lungs in which the exchange of oxygen and carbon dioxide takes place.

amiodarone: An antiarrhythmic drug given during sudden cardiac arrest when the heart does not respond to multiple shocks.

angina: Transient (short-lived) chest discomfort caused by partial or temporary blockage of blood flow to the heart muscle.

anoxia: An absence of oxygen in the tissues.

artifact: A wave on the ECG that results from something other than the electrical activity of the heart.

asystole: A total absence of electrical and mechanical activity in the heart; also called flatline.

atropine: A drug that increases the rate at which the heart paces itself by blocking parasympathetic stimulation to the sinoatrial (SA) node. This drug is used for patients with symptomatic bradycardia or other conduction problems.

automated external defibrillator (AED): A small computerized defibrillator that analyzes electrical signals from the heart to determine when ventricular fibrillation is taking place and then administers a shock to defibrillate the heart.

automated implantable cardiac defibrillator (AICD): A defibrillator placed into patients with either a history of near-death experience or who have been identified as having arrhythmias that are not controlled suitably with medication.

cardiac pacemaker: An electrical device that provides electrical pacing stimulus to a heart that is not pacing itself adequately.

cardiac pharmacology: The study of drugs used in cardiac care and their therapeutic benefits, side effects, and administration.

cardiotoxic: Describes any substance that is harmful or toxic to the heart.

cardioversion: A synchronized countershock used to treat rhythms that still have all the components of a normal cardiac cycle, ie, a P wave, a QRS complex, and a T wave. During a cardioversion, the purpose of synchronizing the shock is to avoid delivering the shock and hitting the top of the T wave, which would, at least in theory, immediately put the patient in ventricular fibrillation resulting in cessation of pumping action.

cerebral embolism: Obstruction of a cerebral artery caused by a clot that was formed elsewhere in the body and traveled to the brain.

cerebral thrombosis: A clot in the brain that results in a blockage called a cerebral embolism.

cerebrovascular accident (CVA): An interruption of blood flow to the brain that results in the loss of brain function; also called stroke or brain attack.

chronotropic: Pertaining to the rate or speed of the heart. A drug with a positive chronotropic effect makes the heart rate speed up. A negative chronotrope slows the heart down.

contraindication: The reason that a certain drug should not be administered to a patient.

defibrillation: The act of shocking a fibrillating (chaotically beating) heart with specialized electrical current in an attempt to restore a normal rhythm.

do not resuscitate orders (DNRs): Written documentation giving permission to medical personnel not to attempt resuscitation in the event of cardiac arrest.

dopamine: An inotropic drug most commonly used to raise a patient's blood pressure, usually administered by IV piggyback, and whose effects are dose dependent.

dosage: The amount of drug that is required to produce the desired therapeutic effect. Dosage usually is stated in grams or portions of grams (for example, grams, milligrams, or micrograms).

drip chamber: The area on the administration set where fluid accumulates so that the tubing remains filled with fluid.

drip set: Another name for an administration set.

dromotropic: Pertaining to the conduction of electricity.

electrocardiogram (ECG): A tracing on graph paper that represents the electrical activity of the heart.

emergency cardiac care: The principles of emergency medicine focused specifically on a patient with a cardiac-oriented problem.

epinephrine: A substance produced by the body (commonly called adrenaline), and a drug produced by pharmaceutical companies that increases pulse rate and blood pressure.

Glasgow Coma Scale: A method of evaluating level of consciousness that uses a scoring system for neurologic responses to specific stimuli.

Good Samaritan laws: Statutory provisions enacted by many states to protect citizens from liability for errors and omissions in giving good faith emergency medical care, unless there is wanton, gross, or willful negligence.

grief: A deep sorrow or mental distress caused by loss, remorse, or affliction.

gtt: A measurement that indicates drops per milliliter.

head tilt-chin lift maneuver: A combination of two movements to open the airway by tilting the forehead back and lifting the chin; used for nontrauma patients.

hemorrhagic stroke: One of the two main types of stroke; occurs as a result of bleeding inside the brain.

hypothermia: A condition in which the internal body temperature falls below 95°F (35°C), usually as a result of prolonged exposure to cool or freezing temperatures.

hypoxia: A dangerous condition in which the body tissues and cells do not have enough oxygen.

implied consent: Type of consent in which a patient who is unable to give consent is given treatment under the legal assumption that he or she would want treatment.

indication: The reason that a certain drug is administered to a patient.

informed consent: Permission given by a competent patient for treatment after the potential risks, benefits, and alternatives to treatment have been explained.

inotropic: Pertaining to the strength with which the heart contracts. A drug with a positive inotropic effect makes the heart beat stronger.

ischemic stroke: One of the two main types of stroke; occurs when blood flow to a particular part of the brain is cut off by a blockage (eg, a clot) inside a blood vessel.

isotonic crystalloids: The main type of fluid used in the prehospital setting for fluid replacement because of its ability to support blood pressure by remaining within the vascular compartment.

jaw-thrust maneuver: Technique to open the airway by placing the fingers behind the angle of the jaw and bringing the jaw forward; used when a patient may have a cervical spine injury.

keep-the-vein-open (KVO) IV set-up: A phrase that refers to the flow rate of a maintenance IV line established as a prophylactic access.

lidocaine: An anesthetic drug used to raise the fibrillation threshold of the heart, suppress frequent premature ventricular contractions, and prevent repeat episodes of ventricular fibrillation.

macrodrip set: An administration set named for the large orifice between the piercing spike and the drip chamber. A macrodrip set allows for rapid fluid flow into the vascular system.

magnesium: A naturally occurring electrolyte in the body; as a drug, it depresses the central nervous system, which may be useful in managing some cases of ventricular fibrillation in which the patient is resistant to conventional therapies.

manual defibrillation: A type of defibrillation in which the electrical countercharge is administered by placing the paddles on the patient's body and holding them there for defibrillation.

microdrip set: An administration set named for the small orifice between the piercing spike and the drip chamber. A microdrip set allows for carefully controlled fluid flow and is ideally suited for medication administration.

morphine: An analgesic drug of choice when rapid anxiety adjustment and pain management are desired.

nitroglycerin: Medication that increases cardiac perfusion by blood flow by causing arteries to dilate; the EMT-B may be allowed to help the patient self-administer the medication.

normal sinus rhythm (NSR): A rhythm that occurs when the electrical activity of the heart and the intervals on the ECG are within normal limits.

oxygen: A gas that cells need in order to metabolize; the heart and brain, especially, cannot function without oxygen.

piercing spike: The hard, sharpened plastic spike on the end of the administration set designed to pierce the sterile membrane of the IV bag.

premature ventricular contractions (PVCs): Contractions of the heart's ventricles that come earlier than normal, often leading to ventricular tachycardia or ventricular fibrillation.

procainamide: A drug similar in its actions to lidocaine, but that must be administered slowly, thereby not making it the drug of first choice in many cardiac emergencies.

pulseless electrical activity (PEA): A rhythm that occurs when there is electrical activity in the heart but no pulse.

reverse triage: A method of managing a mass-casualty incident, in which the dead are treated first, as they may be resuscitated with rescue breathing alone; used in mass-casualty lightning injuries.

route of administration: The method by which a particular drug can be given. Common routes include oral, inhalation, topical, and injection.

Sellick maneuver: A technique used with intubation, in which pressure is applied on either side of the cricoid cartilage to prevent gastric distention and allow better visualization of vocal cords; also called cricoid pressure.

side effect: Expected and predictable effect of a drug that is not part of the therapeutic effect.

sinoatrial node: A collection of specialized electrical cells located high in the upper right corner of the right atrium that is the primary pacemaker of the heart; also called the sinus node.

sinus bradycardia: A common rhythm that is normal except that the rate is slower than normal.

sinus tachycardia: A common rhythm that is normal except that the rate is faster than normal.

splash effect: A situation in which a single strike of lightning injures or kills multiple individuals.

sudden cardiac arrest: A state in which the heart fails to generate an effective and detectable blood flow; pulses are not palpable in cardiac arrest even if muscular and electrical activity continues in the heart.

sympathetic nervous system: The part of the autonomic nervous system responsible for defensive, compensatory responses; often called the fight-or-flight system.

therapeutic effect: The positive, or desirable, effect expected to occur when a drug is administered.

tiered response: Dispatch of both ALS and BLS to the same call. May involve an ALS rendezvous.

tissue plasminogen activator (tPA): A drug that improves neurologic outcomes if given to patients with ischemic stroke within 3 hours of symptom onset.

torsade de pointes: An undulating sinusoidal rhythm in which the axis of the QRS complexes changes from positive to negative and back in a haphazard fashion.

transient ischemic attack (TIA): A disorder of the brain in which brain cells temporarily stop working because of insufficient oxygen, causing stroke-like symptoms that resolve completely within 24 hours of onset.

tricyclic antidepressant (TCA): A class of drug designed to treat depression; when taken in overdose concentrations, these drugs become cardiotoxic.

unstable angina: Angina that involves increasing pain, occurs more frequently, and responds less and less to nitroglycerin.

vasoconstrictive effect: The narrowing of a blood vessel, especially veins and arterioles of the skin.

vasodilatory effect: The widening of a blood vessel.

vasopressin: A hormone that occurs naturally in the body, functioning primarily as an antidiuretic; becomes a potent vasoconstrictor in large doses.

ventricular fibrillation (VF): A rhythm that occurs when the ventricles quiver rather than contract; the most common rhythm in sudden cardiac arrest.

ventricular tachycardia (VT): A rhythm in which the ventricular rate is very fast; the heart is working very hard; may or may not produce a pulse.

Index

Note: Letters following page numbers indicate the following: *d* for definition; *f* for figure; *t* for table; and *tip* for training tip.

ADDITIONAL CREDITS

Unless otherwise indicated, photographs have been supplied by the American Academy of Orthopaedic Surgeons, Jones and Bartlett Publishers, and the Maryland Institute of Emergency Medical Services System. Illustrations are by Nesbitt Graphics and Rolin Graphics.

Chapter 1
Figure 1.4 Adapted from *Basic Life Support for Healthcare Providers,* American Heart Association, 1997. p. 9–2; **Figure 1-5** © Keith Brofsky/ PhotoDisc/Getty Images

Chapter 3
Figure 3.2 Courtesy of Marilyn Westlake

Chapter 4
Figures 4.3, 4.4, 4.5, 4.6, 4.7, 4.9, 4.10, 4.11, 4.12, 4.13 Courtesy of Tomas B. Garcia, MD, FACEP

Chapter 5
Figure 5.2 Adapted from *Basic Life Support for Healthcare Providers,* American Heart Association, 1997. p. 9–2

Chapter 6
Figure 6.14 Courtesy of Matrx

Chapter 7
Figure 7.2 Courtesy of Rhonda Beck

Chapter 9
Figure 9.2A © Spencer Grant/The Picture Cube; **Figure 9.2B** © Bruce Ayres/Getty Images; **Figure 9.2E** © NOAA; **Figure 9.3** © Spencer Grant/Liaison International; **Figure 9.8** © Sean O'Brian, Custom Medical Stock Photography